INVESTING FOR TEENAGERS MADE SIMPLE

YOUR STEP-BY-STEP PATH TO OBTAINING WEALTH AND FINANCIAL FREEDOM QUICKLY

RILEY WEALTH

© **Copyright 2024 - All rights reserved.**

The content contained within this book may not be reproduced, duplicated or transmitted without direct written permission from the author or the publisher.

Under no circumstances will any blame or legal responsibility be held against the publisher, or author, for any damages, reparation, or monetary loss due to the information contained within this book, either directly or indirectly.

Legal Notice:

This book is copyright protected. It is only for personal use. You cannot amend, distribute, sell, use, quote or paraphrase any part, or the content within this book, without the consent of the author or publisher.

Disclaimer Notice:

Please note the information contained within this document is for educational and entertainment purposes only. All effort has been executed to present accurate, up to date, reliable, complete information. No warranties of any kind are declared or implied. Readers acknowledge that the author is not engaged in the rendering of legal, financial, medical or professional advice. The content within this book has been derived from various sources. Please consult a licensed professional before attempting any techniques outlined in this book.

By reading this document, the reader agrees that under no circumstances is the author responsible for any losses, direct or indirect, that are incurred as a result of the use of the information contained within this document, including, but not limited to, errors, omissions, or inaccuracies.

CONTENTS

Introduction   5

1. THE POWER OF STARTING YOUNG   9
   The Early Bird's Advantage   10
   Long-Term Benefits of Starting Early   12
   Setting Your Investment Goals Early   15
   Understanding Compound Interest   22
   How Time Affects the Growth of Your Investments   25
   Tools for Calculating Compound Interest   26

2. ENGAGE WITH FOUNDATIONAL CONCEPTS AND BASIC ASSETS   29
   Creating a Teen-Friendly Budget   29
   The Art of Saving   40
   Budgeting Templates and Resources   44

3. UNDERSTANDING THE STOCK MARKET   47
   The Basics of the Stock Market   48
   How to Read the Stock Market   53
   Glossary   57

4. THE WORLD OF BONDS AND FIXED INCOME INVESTMENT   61
   Understanding Bonds   61
   Risk and Return of Bonds   66
   How Bonds Fit Into Your Investment Portfolio   69
   Stocks vs. Bonds   71

5. EXPLORING MUTUAL FUNDS AND ETFS   73
   What Are Mutual Funds?   73
   Introduction to ETFs   78
   Mutual Fund vs. ETF Comparison   82

6. REAL ESTATE INVESTING FOR TEENS   87
   The Basics   87
   Zeroing In on REITs   92
   Recommended Apps for Investing in REITs   95

7. NAVIGATING CRYPTOCURRENCIES AND
   DIGITAL INVESTMENTS   99
   Introduction to Cryptocurrencies   99
   Buying Cryptocurrencies   103
   Overview of Digital Investing   105
   Checklist Before Investing in Cryptocurrency   108

8. MAKING YOUR FIRST INVESTMENT   109
   How to Open an Investment Account   110
   Understanding Fees and Expenses   113
   Action Step   115

9. RISK MANAGEMENT AND AVOIDING COMMON
   MISTAKES   117
   Understanding Investment Risks   117
   How to Assess and Manage Risk   119
   Risk Management Strategies   120
   Avoiding Common Investing Mistakes   122
   Strategies for Smart Investing   124
   Checklist to Determine Your Personal Risk
   Tolerance Level   125

10. INVESTING AND PLANNING FOR THE FUTURE:
    EDUCATION AND RETIREMENT   127
    Setting Up Education Savings Accounts   127
    Why Investing for Retirement in Your Teens?   130
    Future Savings Calculator   133

    Conclusion   135
    Glossary   139
    References   141

INTRODUCTION

What do you feel when someone says the word "investing" in a conversation? Do you try to change the subject? Do you snooze until the conversation has run its course and someone else changes the subject? Or are you somehow entertained by the idea but can't contribute because you don't know enough? Perhaps you tell yourself, "I'm too young for this; I'll figure it out when the time comes." But what if I tell you that you can start right now? In fact, starting right now would bring you many benefits, such as more money later on or achieving your dreams earlier in life. The point I'm trying to make is that it's never too early to start thinking about finance, and the best time to start is right now!

Unfortunately, many teens think they are too young to start investing or simply have no interest. Now, I know the latter doesn't apply to you, or you wouldn't have picked up this book, right? Just to give you an idea of how common investing is at early ages, 23% of teens between the ages of 13 and 17 have already started investing, and more than 90% of them don't plan to do so in the future (Lin, 2023). So, what about you? Isn't it better to start now since you're going to do it in the future anyway?

Maybe the reason you've picked up this book is that recently had a wake-up call and found out how vital financial knowledge and literacy are. Perhaps some of your peers have started saving and investing, and they are able to do things that you can't. Or maybe you've made a serious financial mistake and want to learn from it. Whatever the reason, you have come to the right place. This is a vital moment in your life. You're about to enter adulthood and want to prepare for it. That's a great decision to make. In the following pages, you will find everything you need, and the jargon will all be explained. I'm going to explain exactly what those complicated words mean, and more importantly, this is going to help you be more confident during those investment conversations. Besides that, you're going to learn about the foundations of investing, how to build long-term wealth, how to deal with economic downturns (you know, when the economy is down and everyone on the news is panicking), and many other things.

But what will all of this bring to you? Well, the earlier you start, the sooner you can reach your goals, whether this is buying your dream house, retiring early, or achieving financial freedom!

Right, so what are we waiting for? Let's get started on your financial journey, shall we? Think of this book as your roadmap into the investing world that will help you build your wealth. Oh, before we start, you don't know who I am or why you should be listening to me. I'm a financial educator and author who understands what you're going through because I was you not that long ago (or at least I think it wasn't too long), and I couldn't find the information I needed to start investing. Everything was scattered around, and the explanations were too difficult to understand. I eventually started to get the hang of things with a lot of trial and error, but it took way longer than it should have. However, you don't have to worry about it because you can find everything you need in the following pages. Alright, now we're ready to start. Let's go!

THE POWER OF STARTING YOUNG

> *The best time to plant a tree was 20 years ago. The second-best time is now.*
>
> — CHINESE PROVERB

You might have heard the saying above before and thought, *Well, 20 years ago, I wasn't even born*. While that might be true, that's not the point of the saying, and being young is certainly an advantage for you. In finances and investment, the earlier you start, the more you have to gain because you have more time to allow your investments to grow. And no, starting as a teenager is not too young at all; it will only allow you to be better off in the future. But before we get into all the technicalities (which I will present very simply, even if this is the first time you open an investment book), let's talk about some teenagers who did start young.

THE EARLY BIRD'S ADVANTAGE

As you might know (or not), an early bird is the name given to someone who does something early, and while this is often associated with waking up early in the morning (don't worry, no one is asking you to do it), in this context, it is about starting early in your investment ventures. Like the following teenagers:

Shehryar Shaukat

Shehryar is one of the most prominent young faces in the business world at the moment, at only 22 years of age. Born in Islamabad in 1995 but raised in Singapore, Shehryar faced some issues when his educational path halted because of a delay in his VISA while pursuing his studies in Canada, but this might have been luck in disguise because he didn't just mope around the house; instead, he dove head first into freelancing, becoming a web developer and earning some money along the way. While he was doing fine as a web developer, he didn't stop there, and his entrepreneurial spirit emerged. He ventured into the stock market, where he made a few successive good investments that yielded impressive returns, particularly an investment in a Chinese manufacturing company called Zhaang Group that solidified his reputation as an investor.

Once again, Shehryat wasn't done exploring and set his sights on the burgeoning world of Bitcoin and cryptocurrency, which allowed him to expand his investments and portfolio further and become a millionaire. Remember, all of this was done by the age of 22, which meant that he started his journey well into his teens.

Brandon Fleisher

Brandon Fleisher is yet another great example of a teen investor who succeeded in this world full of opportunities. In only two years, he tripled his investments from $48,000 to $147,000 at the young age of 17 while in high school. This is a significant benefit, which I will expand on later in the book, is (Morley, 2014). He didn't care much for social media, but he was out there on the internet. Instead of looking at videos of cats, he ran a newsletter and a website in his spare time called the Financial Bulls, where he helped teen investors learn about the stock market, all for free.

Brandon was and still is a confident young man, mainly because he learned, much like you're doing now, about everything related to the stock market, and this was evident upon an investment in a mobile advertising company called Inuvo. Brandon called up Inuvo's CEO, Richard Howe, which, to everyone's surprise, at least at first, Mr. Howe picked up. Here's what Mr. Howe had to say about Brandon: "He would call and ask fairly intelligent and insightful questions even though we thought he was 17 or 17 years old. He really acts as though he's a professional investor" Gillespie (2015). And indeed, he was. He started learning about the stock market at the age of 13, and at that time, his 8th-grade math teacher asked students to pick a stock and follow it to see how it performed. If you think Brandon picked classic choices such as Apple or Microsoft (which are, in no way, bad picks as long as you do your due diligence), he didn't and instead went with Avalon Rare Metals, which later on in the year ended up hitting an all-time high. That was pretty much the beginning of the story of Brandon, the investor because soon after, he started to trade fake stocks (fake in the sense that they are a simulation, which we will talk about later on) and became good enough by that age that his parents co-signed a brokerage account (we will get to that too) and gave him the $48,000 that he then tripled in a couple of years.

LONG-TERM BENEFITS OF STARTING EARLY

There are many benefits to start investing early, and by early, I mean, why not right now? Let me tell you a bit about them. One of the benefits of starting early is that you can start small because you have more time for your investments to grow over time. If you start later on in life, you might have to contribute more money to even come close to the wealth you'd reach if you'd started a few years prior. Also, starting early improves your spending habits because you will have to account for investments in your monthly budget, which is a habit and requires discipline and responsibility when managing your finances. Like everything we start doing early, it becomes second nature to us.

Another necessary benefit, which I will expand on later in the book, is the power of compounding. In a simple way, compounding interest allows you to multiply your investment gains over time. For instance, if you initially invested $1,000 in a 5% annual interest rate compounding account with only a $100 monthly contribution, after 20 years, you'd have over $42,000. If you just had that in your account without any interest, after 20 years, you'd only have $25,000.

The longer your money is invested, the more chances it has to grow faster because the stock market and other types of investments have cycles, and there are periods where they grow faster than others, so the longer your investments, the more chances you have of your money growing faster. The thing with investments is that as long as you don't sell them, they will continue to grow even if you stop contributing.

Another subject that we will explore later on briefly is inflation, where everything, from products to services, gets more expensive over time. Now, if you keep your money in your bank account, where it doesn't grow because everything else will be increasing, your money becomes less valuable. However, when you invest, oftentimes, your money grows faster than inflation does, countering its effects.

How to Stop Procrastinating and Begin Your Investment Adventure

We all procrastinate at some point because we are trying to avoid certain activities that we like a little less. For me, for instance, doing the dishes is when I procrastinate. For many others, especially young investors, it's starting their investment adventure. Now, how can you overcome this procrastination and indecision? Well, while most of it has to come from you, there are a few things you can do to make it easier to take the first step toward starting your investing journey.

For instance, one of the things we tell ourselves is, "I need to wait until I'm ready." Let me tell you that anyone who thinks like that will never be ready in their mind. This is a defensive mechanism we use because we are afraid of taking that step, and if you look closely every time anyone says that or every time you think that way, there's always something in the way that prevents you from making a decision. There's nothing there, really, but your brain will pick on the smallest things and tell you you're not ready. This is, in fact, you making excuses for what you should be doing. Essentially, you have to embrace action over perfection. You can't wait for the perfect moment because that doesn't exist, and it will only delay you from starting things. You have to tell yourself, "There's no perfect time," and start investing. This doesn't mean you shouldn't do research beforehand; you always should, of course.

Another thing that might help you take that first step is to focus on one thing at a time. I know that beginning things, such as investing, can be a little overwhelming. However, the feeling of being overwhelmed will dissipate when you focus on the next step instead of looking at all the other steps you will have to take. Ideally, you should break down what you need to do into more manageable tasks and tackle them one by one. This way, you will also be building momentum and becoming more confident over time.

While I will be discussing this in the next section, establishing specific financial goals will help you stop procrastinating, and it's a little like the point above when breaking down tasks. Here, when you have clear financial goals, you have a direction, and once you have that, the path will be easier to follow.

SETTING YOUR INVESTMENT GOALS EARLY

Setting your investment goals early is one of the most important things you should do. Why? Well, there are several reasons, really. The earlier you start, the higher the chances of success because it gives you a head start, which means your investments have more time to grow, and because of compound interest (which, again, we will talk about later).

Once you get your investment goals sorted, you are more likely to actually focus on the long-term benefits and not the short-term gains. This is because you have a beacon that you can follow, and instead of chasing quick profits, you can strategically plan for the future and look ahead where it really matters.

Types of Financial Goals

Now, short-term gains are not the same as having short-term goals, which you should also have. In fact, there are three types of financial goals that you should pursue because this will keep you motivated to reach those long-term goals. As you might have guessed, the three types of financial goals are short-, medium-, and long-term goals.

Short-term goals are the shortest types of goals, usually lasting between a few weeks or months and a year. These goals could be anything from saving for a nice vacation, building an emergency fund, or saving for a new phone.

Medium-term goals are usually between a year and three or four years and often involve larger purchases, like buying a car, for instance.

Then, there are the long-term goals that extend beyond four years and sometimes might take decades, such as saving for the down payment on a house, saving for retirement, or accumulating a certain amount of wealth.

What to Factor In When Choosing Investment Goals

While there are many options when it comes to where to invest your money, you can still narrow it down to three very important characteristics when analyzing where to put your money. These are: safety, income, and growth. Your goal here is to try and find a balance between these three factors, but let's get to them.

What does safety actually mean? Well, first of all, very few are 100% safe when it comes to investments, as there is no chance of losing money. So, in most of them, you always have that risk, although you can mitigate risks. For instance, bonds (which we will dive into later) are perhaps one of the safest because the government issues them. Anyway, what we need to focus on here is safety, and what you need to understand is that safety comes at a price. Often, the safer an investment is, the lower the returns you will have, or the lower the potential returns, at least. And the opposite is true for riskier investments, where you often have the chance to earn higher returns (gains). So, when choosing your investment goals, you need to look at this risk-return balance, and if you're going for safer investments, it might take a little longer to achieve your goals. Also, you have to keep in mind something we've mentioned before, which is inflation. If your earnings are smaller than the inflation rate, then your money is actually devaluing. But again, you're trying to strike a balance between all three factors, so ideally, you would also have a mix of safer and riskier investments.

The next factor is income, and if you focus on this, then you're focusing on investments that generate fixed income, such as dividend-paying stocks, for instance. While we will talk more about the different types of stocks, for now, all you need to know about dividends is that when you own shares of a company that pays dividends, you will get paid a certain amount per share you own monthly or every quarter, depending on how the company pays their shareholders. Bonds are another type of investment that pays a fixed amount, but what you're looking for here is a steady income that might be a supplement for your other income. While bonds do offer a steady income, they often don't pay as much as certain stocks, so investors who solely focus on income generation might take a little more risk. But of course, you want a balance between these factors, so bonds might be in your portfolio too.

The last factor is capital growth, and this can only be done when you sell an asset, often a stock or stocks. You can only gain by selling if you don't count dividends when you have stocks. However, many different types of capital growth investments go beyond stocks, such as real estate. Right, but what you're looking for here are investments that grow in value over time and that grow your wealth. Stocks are certainly some of the most unpredictable types of capital growth investments because their value can shift quickly. Within the stock world, there are stocks that tend to grow faster, called growth stocks, but there's also volatility (the ups and downs) that you need to be able to stomach.

While the three factors above are the ones you should focus on and try to balance, there are other, smaller factors that you should keep in mind too. One of these is tax mitigation or minimization, where your investment choices might result in you paying less taxes. Here, retirement accounts such as 401(k)s (or RRSP in Canada) or individual retirement accounts (IRAs) can do the job perfectly because they have what are called tax advantages. But anyway, we will get to that. One last smaller factor is the liquidity of your assets, which might factor into an investor's decisions. Essentially, liquidity means how fast your investments can actually be converted into cash with a low risk of loss if you need them. In other words, how fast can you sell an investment and get cash in your hand without losing a large percentage of the investment's value? Bonds are quite liquid because you can sell them quickly and get money into your account fast; so are stocks, although if you're selling them at the wrong time, you might actually lose some of the money invested. On the other hand, real estate is highly illiquid because it takes a long time for you to sell the property (sometimes even months or years) and then some more time to get the actual cash. So, liquidity is just another thing you should keep in mind when choosing your investment goals.

Specific Financial Goals for Teens and How to Set Them

Now that you know the basics about financial goals, how do you actually set them? Before I begin, I want to point out that every single step here will be discussed at length later in the book.

Right, so the first thing you have to do when setting your goals is to create a budget. This is simply a monthly plan for how you're going to allocate your income, such as allocating a part of your income toward essential expenses, saving goals, and so on. There are many budgeting apps that teens can use, such as GoHenry, BusyKid, or Acorn.

Opening a savings account should also be done so you can earn a little interest from the money you set aside (this is usually a small interest rate, like 0.47%, for instance, when compared to other investors, but it's free from risk).

When it comes to setting goals, I will give you a few quick examples of pretty common examples teens have. For instance, when starting to save for college, you should find out how much you will need, such as the cost of tuition, fees, and accommodation (if you will need it). Then, once you know how much you will need and you know your timeline (reach the goal before you enroll in college, at least), you should calculate to find out how much you need to save regularly (say every month) to have the money ready to pay for everything college needs. You can also open a dedicated college savings account such as a Coverdell Education Savings Account (ESA) or a 529 plan (again, don't worry, we will get to this).

Starting to save for retirement is another goal that you should start early, although many teenagers don't really overthink it. Either way, you should consider opening an individual retirement account or, if you're already working, a 401(k) or a RRSP and saving a portion of your income on a regular basis.

Establishing an emergency fund for unexpected expenses or emergencies should also be a priority of yours. It's considered a short-term goal because the aim is to save between three and six months of your income, which you can access in case of an emergency.

This is not different from other savings goals. Add this to your budget so you can allocate a portion to it, and set a timeline so you know exactly how much you have to allocate for it.

SMART Goal Setting

SMART goal setting is an excellent method when it comes to setting financial goals. Let's go through a quick definition before we get to how you can apply it.

SMART goals stand for specific, measurable, achievable, relevant, and time-bound. Now, what does all of this mean? Let's go through the parts.

Specific goals are goals that you have to clearly define. You have to know exactly what these are, not just have an idea of them. For instance, your goal shouldn't just be to save money. Save money for what? How much? You have to answer those calls. Then, there's **measurable**, where you have to quantify your goals so you are able to track them. First, you need to know how much money you will need to get to your goal and then come up with milestones that you can measure through the process of reaching your goal. Say that your goal is $300; you need to find a way of breaking it down into weekly savings, for instance.

Then, we have **achievable goals,** which have to do with setting realistic goals given your current financial situation. You can't expect to save $2,000 a month if your income is $2,000. You have to think about the different factors, such as expenses, income, and everything in between. If you set unachievable goals, you will lose confidence in the whole process. After that, we have **relevant** goals. This means that your goals need to have a purpose that aligns with your values and priorities in the long term. Asking why that particular goal might be important to you in the future is a great way to understand its relevancy. Your goals should have a positive impact on your finances.

Lastly, you have **time-bound** goals where you have to set a deadline to achieve your goals. Without a deadline, you will not be accountable, and you won't be focusing as much on your goals. If you say, I want to save $3,000; eventually, it doesn't have the same ring as saying I'll save $3,000 in six months by saving $500 a month.

Applying SMART Goals

So, now that you know what SMART goals stand for, you need to understand how to apply them. First, you need to create a specific financial goal; the more well-defined it is, the higher the chances you have of reaching your goals. As I've mentioned, if you're setting your goals, you can begin by saying that you need to save more money, and that's a great starting point. But you have to be more specific. How much? For what? For when? You can even go a little further by stating that you want to automate transfers, say 5% of your paycheck, as soon as you get paid toward a savings account or your investment account, for instance.

You also have to come up with ways to measure your progress (this is the measurable part of SMART goals). All goals can be quantified; some might take a little brainstorming to find out, but they all are. Now, say that you want to save for an emergency fund. Here, to make it measurable, you might want to come up with how much you want to save and how often you want to save for that specific goal. Say, I'll automate $100 for my emergency fund every month, for instance.

Of course, as we've seen, you have to ensure that your goals are achievable. A great way to do this is by coming up with specific steps to achieve your goal. If, after drawing the steps, you think things might not be feasible, then they might not be achievable. Say you want to go on vacation with your friends in three months, and you will need $700 to go, which means you will need to save at least $233 every month. However, upon determining your budget, you will find out that you can only save about $150. This is, then, not an achievable goal. At this point, you should have started earlier to ensure you could have saved enough for when the time came.

And, of course, you need to develop a timeline for it. In the example above, the deadline was imposed on us, but this is not always the case, so we might have to impose a timeline so that we can push ourselves to achieve those goals. With self-imposed deadlines, we can work it out better and mold it around our budget, but you still have to set a deadline and not change it unless there's an excellent reason for it.

UNDERSTANDING COMPOUND INTEREST

In simple terms, compound interest allows you to multiply your money over time and at a much faster rate than simple interest, such as in regular savings accounts. Still not convinced? Very well, let's get to it, then. Let me try to explain this in other words before we get to examples. Compound interest is a type of interest that is not only applied to the money you deposit in an account (that's simple interest) but also to the interest you earn over time. So, compound interest works over your deposits and the interest you earn from them too.

How it Works

The best way to explain how compound interest works is by comparing it to simple interest. As I've mentioned above, simple interest only "works" on your deposited amount. Say that you deposit $2,000, and a year later, with simple interest, you've got $2,050, but the interest is only applied to the $2,000 you've deposited. You could leave the money there for years and even reach $3,000; the interest would only be applied to the deposited $2,000. Now, if you deposited more, say $100 more, the interest would be applied to $2,100. But with compound interest, it is different. Say we use the same example where you deposit $2,000, and in the first month, you get $5 interest. In the following month, compound interest won't be applied only to your deposit of $2,000 but to your deposit ($2,000) plus the interest generated that month ($5) and so on. This is why compound interest allows you to multiply your money a lot faster than simple interest would.

While there are many easy-to-use calculators online (just type compound calculator and you'll find them), I think it's important that you still know the formula to calculate compound just in case you, somehow, don't have a calculator at hand. So, the formula is:

$$A = P(1 + r/n)^{(nt)}$$

Where:

- A: is the total amount accumulated over time.
- t: time in years
- P: is the principal amount or the amount you've invested initially (or any other amount invested after the initial investment).
- r: is the annual interest rate

- **n:** is the number of times interest is compounded per year (this could be monthly or annually, usually).

The Rule of 72

This is a straightforward way to calculate how long it will take you to double your investment if the interest in your savings or investment account is somehow fixed annually (if not, you have to come up with an average). Anyway, all you have to do is divide 72 by the annual interest, and you will get an approximate number of years that will take you to double your investment. Say your savings account gives you 5% annual interest. All you have to do is divide 72 by 5 to get, roughly, the number of years needed to double your investment, which in this case would be 14 and a half years. Give it or take. Let's see a few more examples, shall we?

Say that you deposit $1,000 at an interest rate of 10%. With simple interest, after 10 years, you'd have $2,000 since $1,000 plus $1,000 interest. With compound interest, and you can use the formula above to verify this, you'd have around $2,593. Significantly more, don't you think?

Still not convinced? Let's say that you save $100 at an interest rate of 5%, where:

P = $100
r = 5% or 0.05
t = 10 years

So, using the compound interest formula (assuming the compound is annual), then:

A = 100(1+0.05/1)^(1x10)
A = 100(1+0.05)^10

$$A = 100 (1.05)^{10}$$
$$A = 100 (1.62880)$$
$$A = \$162.89$$

HOW TIME AFFECTS THE GROWTH OF YOUR INVESTMENTS

Time is one of the most important aspects when it comes to the growth of your investments, and there are many benefits that come from it, hence the importance of starting early since you have more time.

Time provides you with more control over your investments. How is that done? Well, the longer you have your investment horizon, the more time allows you to ride the ups and downs of the market and benefit from compound interest over time. With more time, you can better adjust your strategies and make better financial decisions. All investments have risks, but time can mitigate some of those risks because it reduces the impact of any short-term fluctuations or volatility in the market. Again, when you invest for the long term, you can ride out the short-term volatility and even take more risks.

As we've seen, time also enhances the power of compound interest. As you know, the longer you have your money invested, the more you will earn. So, as you can see, time is very important when it comes to investments because it helps you increase your gains.

Investment Time Horizon

The investment time horizon is simply a timeline in which you plan to gain value from your investment. When coming up with a time horizon for your investments, these often come from the strategies you choose. Say you want to save for a down payment on a property or save enough for college, and these might be classified as short-, medium-, or long-term goals depending on the time needed to get to them.

As I've mentioned before, investment horizons have different definitions, but it's common to state that short-term investment horizons are anything lasting fewer than five years, medium-term investment horizons are anything between three and five years, and long-term investments are those held for more than 10 or 20 years.

TOOLS FOR CALCULATING COMPOUND INTEREST

There are different ways and tools to calculate compound interest, and one is the fixed formula we've talked about above, but I want to give you the way to do it if you're using a Microsoft Excel sheet, for instance. Using the fixed formula and an Excel sheet, you have to enter "P" (principal) and "i" (annual interest rate), with "n" being the number of periods. If in doubt, just check the above when we talked about compound interest.

So, now you can enter "P" into cell A1, for instance, and enter 1000 into cell B1. Then, you have to add the interest rate on A2 and "0.05" on B2. After that, you have to add the compound periods, which will go to A3 and B3, respectively. On cell B4, you can use the formula: "=(B1x(1+B2)^B3)-B1.

There's another approach to this using an Excel sheet, where first, you have to multiply each year's new balance by the interest rate to come up with compound interest. So, assuming you deposit $1000 in a savings account at a rate of 5% per year, you want to know how much money you will have in five years. So, here, you can type "year" and "balance" into cells A1 and B1, respectively. Then, enter 0 to 5 into cells A2 all the way through A7, and because the

THE POWER OF STARTING YOUNG | 27

balance at the start is $1,000, you should add that to B2. On B3, you should enter "=B2x1.05"; on B4, you should enter B3x1.05 and continue until B7. If you followed this example, you should have $1,276.28 on cell B7, which you will have in five years.

In an actual Excel sheet, it would look something like this:

Year	Balance
0	$100,000.00
1	=B2*1.05
2	=B3*1.05
3	=B4*1.05
4	=B5*1.05
5	=B6*1.05

Finally, let me give you some calculators that you can use to simplify this process:

- **Investor.Gov Compound Interest Calculator:** www.investor.gov/financial-tools-calculators/calculators/compound-interest-calculator
- **TheCalculatorSite.Com Compound Interest Calculator:** www.thecalculatorsite.com/finance/calculators/compoundinterestcalculator.php
- **Counsel for Economic Education Compound Interest Calculator:** econedlink.org/resources/compound-interest-calculator/

With this, we get to the end of the chapter. As we've seen, starting to invest early in life can have tremendous positive consequences, from the ability to start small to taking advantage of the power of compounding. We've discussed a lot here to hopefully convince you to start today! Setting your investments right away is also relevant, and here you have three different types: short-, medium-, and long-term; you should have a mix of these, so you stay motivated to reach your goals.

You can apply SMART goals to better plan your goals and ensure that they are aligned with your values. We then delved into the power of compounding, which is one of the most powerful tools for increasing your wealth. In the following chapter, we will discuss budgeting and saving for your first investment!

ENGAGE WITH FOUNDATIONAL CONCEPTS AND BASIC ASSETS

> *Do not save what is left after spending, but spend what is left after saving.*
>
> — WARREN BUFFETT

Alright, so now that you know why you should start investing early, let's see how you can start saving for your very first investment. Budgeting is the best way to save. This is what we will go through in this chapter: how you can start budgeting, which leads to saving and having money for your very first investment. So, let's start from the beginning: How do I create a budget?

CREATING A TEEN-FRIENDLY BUDGET

First, what is a budget, and why is it so important for you as a teen? I think I've already answered one of the reasons why a budget is so necessary is that you can save enough to invest, of course! But a budget is like a financial plan where you can outline your income, expenses, and any saving goals you might have for a certain period of time (usually a month). Now, a budget brings many benefits to you, especially at this age.

For instance, it helps you develop your financial responsibility. You might think that you are responsible, but until you have a budget, I'm going to say that you are not there yet. While creating a budget is not that hard, the tricky thing here is consistency and following that plan. Also, you will learn to be responsible by prioritizing your spending, understanding the difference between your wants and your needs, and, overall, creating healthy financial habits that you will take with you into adulthood.

Another benefit of budgeting is that it encourages you to save because it "makes" you have to allocate a portion of your income toward your financial goals. As we've seen, these goals can be anything, but what you need to remember is that a budget will keep you accountable for those goals. It also prepares you for adulthood. Some of you might think you're prepared, and you might be in many other aspects of adulthood, but if you don't have a budget, your financial adulthood is not fully developed yet. Learning how to budget prepares you for the financial responsibilities you will have to face as you grow up and how you can deal with expenses such as rent, groceries, utilities, and everything in between.

Many adults fall into this problem where they develop a significant debt, which might be a little hard to get out of. However, with a budget, you can better track your expenses and know when you're overspending, which can help you reduce debt accumulation. The issue nowadays is that spending is increasingly easier; sometimes, all we need is a phone in our hand, and we can pay for everything, but often, we forget to check our accounts. But if you track every single dollar, then you know when you should stop.

And, as you might have guessed, a budget will also help you achieve your financial goals faster by allowing you to prioritize them, regardless of the goals you might have.

Breaking Down Myths and Misconceptions

There are a few things we tend to tell ourselves that often hold us back from successfully creating and following a budget. These things are usually misconceptions, or myths, that you've heard other people say, and somehow you believe you're like them. Let's talk about them.

Alright, so the first misconception, or myth, if you want to call it that, is that budgeting often means depriving yourself. It means you won't be able to eat out, watch a movie in the cinema, or, well, you will never have fun ever again. For some people, this is what they think a budget does to them: it holds them in this prison of boringness for the rest of their lives. But this is not true at all. Will you have to cut some things back? Probably. But a budget is not a prison; if anything, it will help you become freer. Budgeting isn't about deprivation but about allocating your resources wisely to align your finances with the goals you want to achieve. A budget is a roadmap that will help you see the path ahead much clearer; you will know what to prioritize, when you should go out and have fun, and when you shouldn't. It's all about making conscious choices, not depriving yourself of everything worth having.

Right, so another misconception is people telling themselves things like, "I don't need a budget." Well, regardless of how much you earn, everyone needs a budget if they want to reach their goals. Not only does a budget help you track your expenses, but it can also point out areas where you can cut back and, with that, save more. Without a budget, chances are you will overspend, get into debt, and not reach any of your financial goals.

Another, and I must say, popular myth is that you tell yourself that you're not good with numbers. Let me tell you a secret: Most people aren't, but that doesn't stop them from coming up with a great budget. That's why we have calculators and other tools! Also, budgeting does not require you to have a degree in mathematics by any means. It's less about numbers and more about being disciplined and organized. Nowadays, you have many different budgeting apps that can do the heavy lifting for you, such as GoHenry or BusyKid (both of them for teenagers). You just need to practice proper budgeting.

One last myth that I want to talk about is the fact that some teen students believe that if they have enough money, they won't qualify for student aid. The money you have is not the only factor that contributes to your financial aid; there are many other factors, such as educational expenses, family size, assets, income, and so on. If anything, having a budget might improve your situation and even help you qualify for student financial aid by showing that you are financially responsible and have financial needs.

Basics of Budgeting

After all of this, we haven't discussed how you can create a budget, right? Before you start creating it, there are a couple of things you have to go through. The first is understanding your income. Your income is the basis of your budget, and you need to calculate your total monthly income, such as salary, wages, and any other sources of income, regardless of how small they might be. If you pay self-employment taxes (not directly taken from your salary like it happens when you work for someone else), you also have to account for those. Essentially, you have to determine your net income, which is what you actually take home after any taxes (we will get to that later in the book). Most teens don't have to worry about self-employment taxes as of now, so just calculate your take-home money.

The next step is to track your expenses over the same period (again, usually a month). You should also categorize your expenses into fixed expenses, like rent and utility bills, and variable expenses, such as how much you spend on dining out, groceries, and so on. You can check your bank statement to find that out, or at least have a good idea of how much your expenses might be. When you do that, you will have a much better idea of where your money is going.

Now that you have all the necessary information, you can start creating your budget. So, when you begin, start by allocating a portion of your income to your fixed and ongoing expenses, such as rent, utilities, groceries, and so on. Then, allocate some to other expenses, such as dining out, going to the movie theater, and other activities. You have to make sure that the total expenses do not exceed your income. You can use Excel or Google Sheet budgeting templates, where you just need to add the number. Let me give you some great places that you can start from:

1. **Microsoft Excel Budgeting Templates:** create.microsoft.com/en-us/templates/budgets
2. **NerdWallet Budgeting Templates:** www.nerdwallet.com/article/finance/free-budget-spreadsheets-templates
3. **Canva Budget Templates:** www.canva.com/templates/s/budget/

A budget can help you cover your expenses right away, but it should also help you prioritize savings for your financial goals. This means you also have to allocate some of your income to savings accounts and investments (which can be placed in a savings account before investing). It doesn't matter how much you can save; what matters is that you save consistently. Also, a budget is not a static thing that you do for one month and keep it. You have to adjust it from time to time because your financial life is dynamic. You have to regularly review your budget (at least every month) and check on anything that might have changed so you can adjust and maximize your savings.

Tools and Apps to Help You Budget

I've mentioned some budgeting apps above, but let's get into others that not only help you budget but also help you with expense tracking.

You Need a Budget (YNAB) is an excellent one for proactively managing your money. It comes with a price ($14.99 a month), but it's absolutely worth it with all the great insights the app gives you. But as I've said, you need a proactive approach with this app for the best results, so if you're going for it, make sure you commit the time. Now, if you're looking for a simple budgeting app that does most of the heavy lifting, YNAB might not be the one for you. If you're looking for a very comprehensive budgeting app and have the time commitment for it, then look no further.

Wally is a teenager-oriented app with a lot of in-depth information (some might think it might be too much). This app has more features than your average budgeting app, and one crucial feature is bank account integration, so the app does the heavy lifting when it comes to inputting numbers. It's a little cheaper than YNAB at $8.99 a month, and apart from getting used to the different menus, Wally is a great budgeting app.

PocketGuard is another excellent money management app that helps you track your spending, but its feature "In My Pocket" is a delight. This feature tells you exactly how much you can spend, so you don't have to make any calculations. Also, there's a free version, and while it might have some limitations compared to the paid version, it works just fine if you want a simple budgeting app. Besides that, you can personalize reports and sync accounts with many different banks, and it's very easy to build budgets. However, you need to sync your bank account to use it, so if you have no problem with it, then PocketGuard might be ideal for you!

GoodBudget is one of the best budgeting apps for beginners, hands down. It's affordable in the sense that there's a free version, and even the paid version is cheaper than most budgeting apps ($8 per month). It's the most intuitive app on this list so far, and you can get the hang of it quickly. Besides that, it has all the basic features a budgeting app should have, such as tracking expenses or providing you with detailed reports.

Investing and Savings Apps

Let me give you some other apps that you can use for savings and investing. Keep in mind that I'll go in-depth about savings in the next section.

BusyKid is a great savings app that gives you access to a debit card, usually co-signed with your parents or guardian. It has a great feature where your parents, for instance, can assign chores to you, and once completed, they can pay you (handy to start making money helping your parents). It's also extremely easy to use and has plenty of features, including something called the "bucket system," where you can automate allocations so you can stay disciplined. It also has an investment feature where you can start investing for only $10. While it has a 30-day trial, it's $4 a month after that.

FamZoo is a flexible app that allows you to have two different types of accounts. One is a prepaid card where you can add money (or, in this case, your parents can), and you can use it for many different things. The other is the "I Owe You" (IOW) type, where you can record expenses and earnings that your parents or guardian can pay later. Also, you can use a mix of these two types of accounts. When it comes to its features, FamZoo has a lot, from savings goals to savings interest to checklist alerts. The app is comprehensive on this subject. It is also paid, and if you want to pay monthly, it's $5.99, but if you pay 6, 12, or 24 months in advance, it gets a little cheaper.

The last investment and savings app I want to talk about is GoHenry, which also comes with a Visa prepaid debit card, a great mobile app, and the usual features you'd expect in an app of this type, such as setting up regular payments, setting chores, notifications, and more. It costs $4.99 a month per user for the "Every day" membership, but there's also the Plus membership, which costs $2 extra and includes unlimited free top-ups a month (meaning that your parents can add more money to it). The "Everyday" membership only allows one free top-up per month.

Tips for Sticking to Your Budget

At the beginning of your budget creation journey, things might not look all that easy. You might be a little overwhelmed, and that's why I'm going to give you some tips on how you can stick to your budget.

First of all, to get into the habit of creating a budget every month, the first thing I have to say is to keep it simple. Overcomplicating things at this stage won't motivate you. Begin with your long-term goals because those are unlikely to change anytime soon, and then move on to medium- and short-term goals. The truth is, you might have to go through a little trial and error to really figure out how much you can save.

There are many different budgeting methods, and it might be a good idea to try a few different ones and see which one works best for you. I'm going to explain a few that might be ideal for you at this stage. A popular one is the 50/30/20 rule, where you allocate your income according to the percentage above. So, 50% of your income should go toward your needs, such as rent, groceries, utilities, and everything else you need to pay to survive. 30% of your income should go to your wants, which means dining out, going to the cinema, buying clothes, and anything else you might want to spend your money on. The last 20% goes toward saving goals (including investments). Now, 30% of your money going to wants might seem a lot, and it certainly is, but when you're just starting out and trying to stick to your budget, you might have to give yourself a break, and this budgeting method is a nice and easy one to start with.

Another budgeting method I want to talk to you about is the zero-budgeting approach. Essentially, with this method, every single dollar has to have a purpose, and you have to allocate it until you have nothing in your checking account. In other words, you have to have a plan for all of your income. Again, you should start by allocating part of your income toward your needs, then set aside money for your savings and keep adjusting your budget until there's nothing left in your account.

One last one I want to talk about is the "pay-yourself-first" approach. As the name indicates, with this budgeting strategy, you prioritize your savings before you allocate money toward the rest of your expenses. This way, you know you're going to reach your financial goals faster.

Continuing with some other tips, does the sentence "Save first, spend later mean anything to you?" Well, this simply means that you should try to prioritize your savings, just like with the pay-yourself-first approach. Essentially, you can treat savings as a non-negotiable expense or a need. By automating savings, you can make sure that you can reach your goals. You should also focus on your needs, not your wants. For this, you need to understand the distinction well enough and, above all, have self-control. If you do this and prioritize spending on needs over wants, you can make sure that your essential expenses are covered.

As I've mentioned before, knowing exactly how much money is coming in and tracking your expenses at all times allows you to stay informed about your money and make better financial choices. Besides that, regularly reviewing your transactions will allow you to spot anything that might not be right and cut back on unnecessary expenses. One thing that teenagers have to go through more than adults do is peer pressure. You shouldn't, under no circumstances, give in to peer pressure. I know you want your friends to like you, but remember that you have goals, and you need to stay on track and not spend money if it's not calculated.

And a little secret: if they are really your friends, they will be okay with you saying no to a dinner out once in a while.

Regardless of how much you are and will continue to learn in this book or from any other sources on the web, chances are that, especially at the beginning, you might make some mistakes, and that's totally fine as long as you learn from your mistakes. When you make a mistake, you should be able to analyze and find out where things went wrong so you don't fall for it the next time.

One last thing when it comes to making your budget creation a little easier is to involve your parents. They've been through it and can help you navigate and guide you.

THE ART OF SAVING

Did you know that saving is an art? Yes, many people don't know that, and while it is an art, there are still some steps you need to go through, especially when it comes to saving money as a teenager. So, let's go through those essential steps. The first thing you have to do is open a savings account, obviously.

Opening a Savings Account

It's not only about opening an account; it's about opening the right account for you. In this particular case, you should try to pick one that fits your lifestyle, such as a teen-designed account. Now, there are a lot to choose from, so I'm just going to point out a few, but you still have to do your research. Also, another thing to keep in mind is that some banks only allow you to open a savings account if you already have a checking account with them.

The M&T Starter Savings Account by M&T Bank is a good one to start with. While it has a low-interest rate of 0.01%, there's no minimum deposit requirement or monthly maintenance fee. Besides that, it also comes with automated saving tools and a debit card that you can use. The Northpointe Bank Kids Savings offers much better annual interest with up to 1.50%, but this only affects the first $1,000 you deposit, and any other deposits you make after that go down to 1.12%, which is not too bad. Credit unions often offer better rates; however, the requirement to open an account there is a lot more stringent, and unless your parents have an account with one credit union, chances are you will not be able to open a bank account there. However, it's worth mentioning it to your parents. Another thing worth checking before you decide on your bank account is its extra features, such as good and easy access to online banking, a great mobile app, and so on.

Anyway, after you've analyzed and picked the right bank account for you and before you actually open it, you will need to gather some specific documents. Things such as a government-issued ID, proof of address, and social security number are usually what's required. When you've done all of the above, it's time to contact the bank to actually open the account. Here, you can either do it online or in-branch, but keep in mind that online banks don't have branches, so your only alternative is to register online. Brick-and-mortar banks might give you the option to complete your application by going to the nearest branch or by doing it online. There's no significant difference here, and it's all up to you.

Once your account is open, certain banks prompt you to make an instant initial deposit; others don't require you to do one right away, but it's good practice to fund your account sooner rather than later. Make sure you set up your account features, such as customizing your account settings the way you prefer, and so on.

How to Save

I'm sure you already know this, but I can't emphasize enough how important this is. When you want to save and work toward your financial goals, you need to set them first. Without them, everything else in your financial life gets more difficult. It doesn't matter what those savings are as long as you set them and prioritize them. Another thing I prompt you to do is to break down larger goals into smaller ones that you can manage better.

As I've already mentioned in the budgeting section, tracking your spending is a way to reach your financial goals faster. You can use some of the budgeting techniques we've talked about earlier. Again, review your budget and your financial transactions on a regular basis to ensure that your spending aligns with your savings goals. You also have to separate your spending money from your savings money. This often means having two separate accounts or having different pots where you allocate your income to have this division. This will help you not dip into your savings, even if you accidentally do so.

With all of this tracking, you have the chance to cut back on expenses because you now know exactly where your money is going and what can be cut from your expenses, freeing up more of your funds for savings. As I've said before, automating your savings means that when you receive your income, a predetermined portion goes to your savings right away, so you know you are consistently saving before spending.

Other than that, you can always look for ways to earn more money. There are many ways you can do this, whether it is through part-time jobs, freelancing gigs, and so on. I will give you some practical suggestions at the end of the chapter.

Importance of an Emergency Fund and How to Build One

An emergency fund is money you set aside for a rainy day, an unexpected expense, such as a medical bill, or any other financial emergency. Why? Well, this way, you don't have to spend money from your savings and possibly delay your saving goals. An emergency fund is a cushion you can use without disturbing your budget. It's also a way to protect you from financial distress by offering you stability, which allows you to go through any emergency without the added financial stress these situations might bring. As I've said, it also helps you preserve your savings and your investments because, without it, you might be forced to use some of your savings, or worse, sell your investments, to pay for that emergency. But how do you build it?

Well, first, you need to figure out how much you should save. There is no right answer here; however, there are a few common answers. Some specialists state that three months of expenses is enough; others say six months of expenses. So, anything in between is a great start; the exact amount is up to you as long as you determine the amount you want to reach. Starting small is fine; in fact, that is what most people do. A modest amount can go a long way if you are consistent in your contributions to your emergency fund. It's crucial that you keep your emergency fund separate from your savings and your checking account and that you make it easily accessible so you can use it quickly if you need it.

You can always open a new bank account so you know that you can get to it quickly, and that it is secure. As I've mentioned before, automating transfers is vital because you will never forget to add to your fund. As with everything we've seen so far, monitoring and adjusting your contributions to your savings account is essential so you are on top of what is happening. Also, life is constantly changing, so you should change the size of your emergency fund according to the changes in your life.

BUDGETING TEMPLATES AND RESOURCES

Alright, so let me give you a very basic template that you can use:

Monthly Income	Amount ($)
Wages or Salary	
Interest Savings or Investment Income	
Other Income	
Total Monthly Income	
Monthly Expenses	Amount ($)
Housing (mortgage or rent)	
Utilities	
Groceries	
Transportation	
Leisure	
Savings and Investments	
Total Monthly Expenses	
Summary	Amount ($)
Total Monthly Income	
Total Monthly Expenses	
Remaining	

I've provided more budgeting templates while discussing budgets earlier that you can use. Now, let's explore some different ways you can earn money as a teen. Let me separate this into two categories: traditional and digital ways of earning money as a teenager. Starting with traditional methods, car care is a popular one where you can perform a few tasks on your neighbors or your family's cars, such as washing, for instance. If there are any farms around your house or if you know someone who has a farm, you can ask them to assist them in planting, harvesting, or even taking care of farm animals. Babysitting or pet sitting is also popular among teenagers, and if you like animals, it might be exactly what you need! There's also working part-time in the food industry, such as in restaurants or coffee shops, or as a retail worker in clothing stores or supermarkets.

When it comes to digital or virtual ways of earning money, there's also a large array of options here. Freelancing, such as freelance writing, graphic design, marketing, content creation, social media management, and more, are great ways to make some extra money without leaving your house. If you know a thing or two about computers or IT, then programming or web development might be more appropriate for you. If you prefer administrative work, data entry or becoming a virtual assistant can be a great part-time job.

Lastly, tutoring can be done offline or online, and if you're good at a particular subject, you can earn a bit of money. You can offer tutoring services to students who might need extra help with exams or their studies in general. Above all, these types of jobs will give you great experience when you enter adulthood.

Right, so now you know how important budgeting is when it comes to saving not only for you but also for your first investment. The first thing we looked at was how you can create a budget and what apps you can use to make it easier to stay on track. Then, we looked at savings in general and their importance in your personal finances. This is relevant because you need to have a great financial foundation before you venture into investments, which is what we will be exploring in the following chapter, where we will focus on understanding the stock market.

UNDERSTANDING THE STOCK MARKET

> *The stock market is filled with individuals who know the price of everything but the value of nothing.*
>
> — PHILIP FISHER

When we begin our venture into the world of investments, we sometimes feel haunted by the mere sound of the word "stock market." Well, this chapter will simplify the whole thing for you and demystify some of the things you might have heard, such as "The stock market is for wealthy people" or "You lose more than you win in the stock market." This is often said by people who either have not invested in the stock market or did it for a short period, didn't go well, and made up their minds about how horrible the stock market is. It's not, and we will see why, but let me just emphasize this once again: while there are investors who make risky *bets* in the stock market and sometimes can double their money in just a few days, this is not what I'm teaching in this book. The stock market is not a casino; it's a place where wealth grows gradually and exponentially the longer you leave your money there. It's not a get-rich-quick type of thing. Here, I'll share invaluable insights on how you can become successful and build wealth through the stock market.

THE BASICS OF THE STOCK MARKET

Let's look at the basics of the stock market before moving forward to more (but not really) complex ideas. The stock market is a place where you can exchange stock shares and other publicly held financial securities of companies. Now, the stock market serves another purpose and is a vital part of a free-market economy. Essentially, a free-market economy is an economic system with very little or no government interference and based on competition. Now, why is the stock market so important for it? There are a few reasons for that. One is capital allocation, in this case, funds, which makes it easier for investors and businesses to connect and the latter to raise funds for their operations. In turn, investors, by buying shares, fuel economic growth and innovation and, of course, generate wealth for themselves. It's also an efficient price mechanism because the buying and selling of securities leads to fair (or fairer) market prices based on supply and demand, and because of it, most of the time, the stock market reflects the intrinsic value (the real value of a company or asset) and makes the market more efficient. For investors, participating in the stock market means the creation of wealth, or at least the opportunity to do so. Furthermore, the stock market also allows the distribution of wealth since some companies either pay dividends or reinvest profits.

As I've mentioned above, publicly traded companies issue shares to raise funds without the need to get into debt through business loans. To do this, they sell ownership stakes to investors like you so they have capital to continue their operations. Price shares are determined based on supply and demand. So, if there's a lot of interest in buying a particular stock, the price goes up. If the opposite is true, then the price goes down. Although this is a very simplistic way of putting things, supply and demand are affected by other factors such as the country's overall economic conditions, trends in the industry, the company's performance, and, of course, the investor's sentiment about a certain stock or company.

While you might be more familiar with the New York Stock Exchange (NYSE), one of the largest stock exchanges, many others exist within and outside the US. For instance, the London Stock Exchange (LSE) and the Tokyo Stock Exchange (TSE) are some of the other more significant stock exchanges.

Types of Stocks

There are a few different types of stocks, and while some have clear definitions, others do not, and some stocks might even accommodate two different types.

Let's start with common and preferred stocks. Common stocks represent ownership and might even give you voting rights in a company's matters. Another particularity of common stock is the possibility of receiving dividends; however, investors with preferred stocks have fixed dividends, which have higher rates than the dividends from common stocks. In other words, preferred stocks have priority over common stocks when it comes to receiving dividends, and in case the company liquidates (sells for cash) assets, preferred stock investors also have priority over common stockholders, but they don't have voting rights. While companies might issue preferred and common stocks, the latter is far more common on the stock exchange.

Then there are growth and value stocks, and here, the line separating them is not as defined, but with some research on the companies, you can figure out one and the other. So, growth stocks are shares of companies expected to grow faster than the average of the stock market (for instance, the S&P 500). Investors that invest in these types of stocks are aiming for the potential for an increase in the capital appreciation of that company, and often, these stocks don't pay dividends since they prefer to reinvest them back into the company, so the price of their stock continues to grow. Value stocks are shares of companies that might be considered undervalued when compared to their actual value. Of course, you need to do your research here to try to determine that (which we will be talking about later on in the book).

Dividend and non-dividend stocks are easy to spot and have clear definitions. Dividend stocks are companies that distribute a part of their earnings to their investors, and if you are an investor who is looking for a fixed income, then dividend stocks might be ideal. Income stocks, which is another definition you might hear, are dividend-paying stocks, and often, these companies are stable and have a great dividend-paying history. Blue-chip stocks are the stocks of large and stable companies, which are often the market leaders in their industries. As you might have guessed, they often pay dividends as well. Non-dividend stocks, like the growth stocks we've seen above, don't pay dividends and prefer to reinvest any earnings into the company.

Right, then, there are cyclical and non-cyclical stocks that might also fall into some of the categories I've mentioned above. Essentially, the economy runs in cycles where there's an expansion (relatively rapid growth, lower interest rates, etc.), followed by the peak when growth hits the highest, then a contraction or a correction where the economic growth slows down (here you might see an increase in unemployment, for instance), and lastly the trough of the cycle where the economy reaches its lowest point. Now, some company stocks follow this exact cycle, which is closely tied to the economic cycle, where they grow and fall at the same time. Non-cyclical stocks don't follow this cycle and oftentimes perform well regardless of what is happening in the economy in general.

I want to talk about two other different types of stocks. The first is an initial public offering (IPO) stock, which simply refers to the shares of a company that is entering the stock market, moving from being a privately traded company to a publicly traded company for the very first time. Think of it as a debut on the stock market. While there's a lot to be said about IPOs, I'm not going too deep into them because their success depends on many different factors, and while they need to disclose their financials publicly, there's not as much information available at the time the company debuts in the stock market.

The last type of stock I want to talk about is penny stocks. As per definition, penny stocks are shares of small companies that trade below $5 per share. While not always true, these stocks tend to be volatile, which makes them a risky investment, and they are more often found during the early years of a company in the stock market.

Understanding Dividends

While the concept of dividends is straightforward, there are a few things that you need to know about them. As you know, dividends are distributions or payments by a company to its shareholders (investors like you). This usually comes in the form of cash or, more rarely, in the form of more shares as part of the company's earnings distribution. Essentially, when a company gets its earnings, a part of it goes to its shareholders. They do this as a way to share their rewards with shareholders who invest in them, but it's also a way to bring in more investors who aim to attain some fixed income from their investments. So, you can also see dividends as an incentive for investors to continue to hold on to their shares and bring in new investors. But how are dividend amounts determined?

Well, the amount to pay to shareholders is all on the company's board of directors. They are the ones who decide how much shareholders should get paid per share, but there are some factors that influence this decision. For instance, the company's performance and profitability have an impact on the amount received by shareholders. Now, there's one thing you need to understand about dividends, and these are their dates. Different companies pay dividends regularly, but the number of times in a year depends. For example, some companies might pay dividends every three months, others might pay every month, or others might even pay once every year. Now, whenever that happens, the board of directors always announces when and how much they will be paying investors. So, the key dates you should be looking out for are the declaration date, when the company announces its intention to pay dividends, and the record date, which is the date on which you, the shareholder, have to hold shares so this can be recorded and you receive the dividend. Then, there's the ex-dividend date, which is when the stock begins to trade without the dividend, so if you purchase shares on or after this date, you won't receive the upcoming dividend. It's also true that if you held shares before the ex-dividend date and then sold them, you are still entitled to receive the upcoming dividend even if you no longer hold shares of that company. Then there's the payment date, which is when you actually get paid the dividend straight into your brokerage account.

Some of the most popular and highest-paying dividend stocks are Procter & Gamble (PG), Coca-Cola (KO), and Johnson & Johnson (JNJ). While the dividend amount might change, historically, these companies have offered great dividend rates to their shareholders. Other companies, such as Apple or Microsoft, pay dividends, but usually not as much as the companies above; however, they also tend to grow their share price over time more than the companies above, so they are sort of hybrid companies where you receive dividends while also potentially increasing their share price.

HOW TO READ THE STOCK MARKET

Another intimidating thing about the stock market for those who are just starting out is the charts. What do they even mean, right? Well, you actually get some interesting information just by looking at different stock charts. In fact, knowing how to read stock market charts is absolutely essential for you as an investor so you can better analyze market trends, spot patterns, and make better decisions. Think of them as a neat visual representation of the confusing numbers, and you can better track the performance of the different stocks and identify opportunities faster.

Let's get to the terms you might encounter when analyzing a stock chart. Some of the terms that are usually seen together are "open," "high," "low," and "previous close." These are actually easy to get. Open simply means the price at which a certain stock price opens when the stock exchange opens. High is the highest price point during a day, a week, a month, a year, and so on, depending on the specific period you are looking at. Low is the opposite of high, and the previous close is the closing price of a stock on the day before.

You might have also come across other terms that you didn't get, such as market cap, PE ratio, dividend yield, or 52-week high and low. Right, so the market cap stands for market capitalization and tells you the total value of the outstanding shares (shares not bought by investors at that time). You can get to the market cap number by multiplying the current stock price of a given stock by the number of outstanding shares (these are publicly displayed figures). This essentially tells you what that specific company is worth, but we will get into that later, and the same goes for some of the following definitions: The price-to-earnings ratio (PE ratio) is a measure where you can find out the valuation of a company. You can get to this number by dividing the current stock price of a given stock by its earnings per share (EPS). The dividend yield is the percentage paid out to you annually (keep in mind that some companies pay monthly or quarterly, but the dividend yield usually reflects the annual payout). The 52-week high and low, as you might have guessed, is the highest and lowest price point during the year (last 52 weeks).

There are other, a little more advanced, stock market chart terms that you will fully understand later, but I'll leave you with a basic definition for now. The "bid and ask" term tells you the highest price that an investor who is buying is willing to pay for a share of a certain stock, and well, the lowest is the same thing but the lowest price point a seller is willing to accept for a certain stock.

Another term you might come across is moving averages, which is simply a technique used to find the average of stock price fluctuations. It's great if you want to find a trend in a certain stock, and you can calculate it as you calculate the average of anything else by looking at the average closing prices over a certain period. Lastly, the 1-year target estimate is nothing but a projection done by analysts where they think the stock price might be in the next 12 months, and this is based on both the technical and the fundamental analysis (remember them?).

Understanding Market Indices

Market indices such as the S&P 500 or Nasdaq can be considered benchmarks of the overall performance of a certain market segment; for instance, the Nasdaq follows or is focused on high-technology companies. Others, like the S&P 500, focus on the entire market by tracking the performance of the 500 largest US companies. You can use these benchmarks to track the performance of aspects of the market, understand investors' sentiments, or even compare them with their own portfolios to determine if you have outperformed the market or not. Besides that, market indexes can provide you with great insights into the volatility or current market trends.

Now, how can you read stock market indexes? Well, it's just like reading any other stock chart, with the particularity that when you look at the charts, you are looking at a weighted average of the prices of all the stocks that the index has. Now, keep in mind that not all stocks in an index weigh the same, meaning that indexes might have a higher percentage of their portfolio allocated to certain stocks than others. Anyway, without looking at this, you can interpret any changes in the value of indexes to check if there was any change in investors' sentiment or try to understand which direction it might go. In general, if you see a rise in index values, this might tell you that there might be a bullish sentiment (going up) from investors, while a decline might mean a bearish sentiment (going down). However, this is just an indicator; there are other things that you need to look at to determine the direction of the market. You can use some of the techniques we've talked about to try and identify trends and patterns, just like in a regular stock.

The Significance of Market News and Events

Now, news and events related to the market can have a massive influence on the price of stocks or the market in general. So, things like economic reports, earnings announcements, or even geopolitical changes might have an impact. And while positive news might bring the demand for a stock up, which consequently raises the price of that stock, bad news might have the opposite effect. However, the nature of the news and how investors perceive it changes mainly due to the relevance of the news to the stock or sector. For instance, more stringent government regulations on the tech industry might mean that tech industry stocks might go down. News and events might also have an impact on investors' confidence and behavior, and here, good news might bring more confidence to investors and more interest in specific stocks; bad news might have the opposite effect, and investors might sell their investments, which might bring the stock price of a given company down.

So, with this, what I mean to say is that staying informed is absolutely critical when you're an investor. Oftentimes, this reaction by investors to good or bad news is, well, an overreaction, and the stock goes back up or down to its previous price, but nonetheless, you need to follow developments in different sectors and specific companies to understand how they might affect your portfolio.

GLOSSARY

Let me give you some other words you might hear as you navigate the investment world.

Bear and bull markets: I've already mentioned these, but let me give you a more extensive definition. A bear market is defined by an extended period of decline in the overall stock market (price-wise) and where there's pessimism from the investors as well as uncertainty. During this time, most investors expect to lose some of their wealth in the stock or sell off to mitigate those losses. A bull market is the opposite and happens when there's a prolonged rise in stock prices where investors are more optimistic, and the economy is stronger, which results in the gain of wealth.

Another term that is often used is dollar-cost-averaging, which is simply an investment strategy that we will discuss later. But to give you an idea of how it works, it essentially consists of investing a fixed amount of money at regular intervals without caring about market conditions. This way, the prices of your shares are averaged, which reduces the price over time.

You're familiar with volatility, which is a certain stock's fluctuation. When investors refer to a stock with high volatility, they are stating that the price of that particular stock is unstable. Low volatility means there are fewer ups and downs in the price of the stock. I've also mentioned liquidity before, and here, it simply refers to how easy it is to transform an asset such as stocks into cash without significantly impacting its price. Risk tolerance is the degree of potential loss you are willing to endure when investing. If you are ready to lose a significant amount of money in exchange for the potential of higher returns, then you might have a high-risk tolerance, for instance.

Lastly, at least for the terms that matter now, there's the annual report. These are financial documents that publicly traded companies have to make public for their shareholders to analyze. These reports give great insights into the company's performance and are an important part of an investor's analysis.

This is all you need to know to begin to understand the stock market. We've looked at the basics and the different types of stocks you can come across, as well as how you can read those seemingly confusing stock market charts, which you found out are not that hard to understand. Lastly, we talked about the importance of market indexes, how to understand them, and the impact of market news and events on stock prices. Here are some teen-friendly investment apps:

- Acorn
- Robinhood
- Stash
- Greenlight

In the following chapter, we will go through a different facet of investments and delve into bonds and fixed-income investments!

THE WORLD OF BONDS AND FIXED INCOME INVESTMENT

Bonds are not only for rich investors; they're for anyone who wants a safer way to grow their money. But what are bonds, exactly? Well, first of all, there's no relation between bonds in finance and Bond the movie, but they are just as interesting from an investor's point of view, at least.

UNDERSTANDING BONDS

From a formal definition, bonds are securities issued by governments, corporations, or municipalities. Now, this might not tell you a lot, right? In other words, bonds are loans where you, the bondholder, act as the lender. Yes, I'm saying that governments and companies "ask" for money through bonds. When you purchase a bond, you are essentially lending money to the issuer of the bond, where you get regular interest, called coupons, and once the bond matures (at the end of the loan), you get your money back.

So, as I've mentioned above, bonds have a predetermined maturity date where the bond issuer, whether it's a government, a company, or a municipality, pays you back the money you've invested in the bond, and until the maturity date, you receive interest payments. Sounds like a good deal, right? Well, it is, but usually, the interest paid is not as high as the average of what one would get in the stock market; however, bonds are a lot less risky. The prices of bonds tend to fluctuate depending on the changes in interest rates, how creditworthy the bond issuer is, and overall market conditions at the time.

The Benefits of Bonds

Well, besides the benefits I've talked about above, bonds have a few things working for them. For instance, income generation, of course. You know for sure that you will receive interest payments on a regular basis (although the number of times you receive interest payments a year depends on the bond). So, if you're an income-oriented investor, bonds are a great investment.

Bonds are also a great way to diversify your portfolio, which we will talk about a little more later. Diversification is a strategy to mitigate the risks of investments, and since bonds have a much lower risk, they are often welcome in most investor portfolios. Lastly, they also preserve capital, especially those issued by governments, since they not only preserve capital by paying you back the full amount you've invested, but you also earn income.

Characteristics of Bonds

Now, bonds might have some unusual definitions that you will certainly come across when doing your research. Maturity date is one of those terms, but I've mentioned it briefly above. Essentially, this is the date on which the bond issuer repays you the money you've invested in the bond. Now, bonds have different lengths. There are short-term bonds, which usually last less than a year; intermediate-term bonds, between one and 10 years; and long-term bonds, which last over 10 years to mature. The coupon rate is the interest rate payment you receive from the bond issuer, which is usually a percentage of the bond's price. Face value is the price you've paid for the bond, or, in other words, what you've lent to the bond issuer, as well as the amount you receive once the bond hits the maturity date.

How Do I Buy Bonds?

There are several ways to buy bonds, such as through banks, brokerage companies, or online trading platforms. United States Treasury bonds, or government bonds, can be bought directly from the government's website, TreasuryDirect.gov.

Types of Bonds

So, now, let's dive into the different types of bonds. Let's begin with the ones I've mentioned previously since these are also the most common ones.

Governments or Treasury bonds are the safest bonds out there, which means they don't default. In other words, they always pay the principal upon maturity date. Other bonds, while not common, might default if, for instance, a company (in the case of corporate bonds) doesn't have money to pay them back. When it comes to its interest rates, while they vary, they are fixed throughout the bond's life and can range from short- to long-term. Again, they are low-risk but also low in returns, which means their interest rate is often low when compared to other types of bonds.

Corporate bonds are issued by companies when they need to raise capital for their operations. They tend to offer higher rates than Treasury bonds, but the risk of default on the corporation's behalf is also higher. Although you need to research the company to understand its creditworthiness, remember that while these are more risky than government bonds, they are less risky than stocks (at least on average).

Municipal bonds are also low-risk, and the local government or state that issues them often raises money for infrastructure such as roads or hospitals. One thing to note here is that municipal bonds' interest payments are often tax-exempt, meaning that you might not need to pay tax on your gains, which adds to their benefits.

Then, there are agency bonds issued by companies sponsored by governments, which might give them more creditworthiness. Because of that, their interest rates are usually a little higher than government bonds but lower than corporate bonds. Emerging market bonds can be issued by corporations or governments in developing economies. While they offer higher interest rates, there's more risk associated with them because of the underlying emerging economy. Mortgage-backed and asset-backed bonds are issued by financial companies and backed by either mortgages or different types of assets like credit cards, auto loans, or even student loans. Here, you might find higher interest-rate payments, but there's also more risk. Lastly, we have green bonds, which fall under corporations, municipalities, or government bonds, but the money raised is exclusively used for environmentally friendly projects. If this is something that you want to be part of, then green bonds might be a great way to invest in something that you want to back up. Plus, because different organizations and governments issue them, you can pick the level of risk.

How to Make Money from Bonds?

You can make money with bonds in two ways: coupon-paying bonds and zero-coupon bonds.

In a coupon-paying bond, you buy the bond directly from the issuer and hold it until the maturity date so you can earn interest payments. Bonds can also be bought and sold in a secondary market within their maturity date by exchanging them with other bondholders, and here, bonds are sold at a discount when compared to their initial face value. This is because if you buy an existing bond, you will not get as much money from interest rate payments.

There are also zero-coupon bonds, where the investors don't receive any interest payments until the bond matures. If you buy a bond in the secondary market, you often buy it at a discount compared to its face value. While some bonds have a preset face value, which means you will receive a preset amount of money at maturity, there are other bonds that have inflation indexes, and the amount paid at maturity is defined at the maturity date and based on factors such as the consumer price index.

Bond Strategies

When it comes to the strategies used when investing in bonds, we can divide them into passive and active strategies. The most common passive strategy is buy and hold, where you buy a bond directly from the issuer and hold it until maturity, and in the meantime, you collect interest payments. Bond indexing is also a passive bond strategy where you try to mimic the performance of bond indexes, much like the stock indexes we've mentioned before. For instance, the Bloomberg Barclays U.S. Aggregate Bond Index is a popular one where you buy bonds that might be in this particular index and try to match their return without mitigating transaction costs.

When it comes to active strategies, investors who choose this strategy aim to outperform bond indexes. One of the most common strategies here is sector rotation, where you actively allocate bond holdings across different sectors, like municipal, government, and corporate bonds, based on the current market conditions. Credit quality allocation happens when investors try to identify individual bonds that might increase in price because of the bond issuer's credit. However, you should know that active strategies are often used together.

RISK AND RETURN OF BONDS

While bonds are considered one of the safest investments you can find (and indeed they are), they still have some risks for you to understand. Let's go through them.

Right, so there's the interest rate risk, which is the most significant risk when it comes to bonds because it might affect your returns. In this case, it refers to the potential for the interest rate of a bond to fluctuate, so you won't always get the same amount of interest payments. This happens when interest rates rise in the economy, which prompts the issuing of newer bonds with a higher interest rate and makes existing bonds a little less attractive because they have lower interest rates. The exception to this is zero-coupon bonds, where you get interest payments at maturity and are sensitive to interest rate changes, so you can either get more or less at maturity depending on the changes in interest rates, while regular bonds tend to have a fixed rate. So, just to make it clear, most bonds have a fixed interest rate, but the problem here is that between the time the bond matures, the interest rates might go up, and your fixed-rate bond continues the same while new bonds are issued with higher interest rates.

Credit risk, or default risk, is also something you have to consider. Essentially, this is the risk of the bond issuer not being able to pay you interest payments or to pay you back the premium as promised. This is where creditworthiness comes in. Companies that have low creditworthiness have higher chances of defaulting on their obligations, but they also offer higher interest rates. The exception here is Treasury bonds, where the U.S. government has never defaulted on its obligations, so they are virtually risk-free.

The reinvestment risk happens when you get interest payments from your bonds and have to reinvest them at current market rates. The issue here is that the current market rates might be lower than the original rates of the bond. If this is the case, then you might lower your returns as time goes on. Inflation risk is another one, but in this case, if you have fixed-rate bonds, this is more likely to happen. Inflation is the rate at which the prices of goods and services increase. So, groceries, your Spotify and

Netflix subscriptions, and everything else gets more expensive by a certain percentage, and because you have a fixed-interest bond, your interest payments remain the same, which means that they are worth less as everything gets more expensive. In other words, the value of your bond's interest rate is lower, especially if inflation exceeds your bond's yield.

Then, we have liquidity risk, and this has to do with how easily you can purchase or sell bonds in the market without impacting the price of the bonds you buy or sell. So, for instance, bonds that have less liquidity might have a higher volatility in price, which means if you're buying, they might get more expensive, and if you're selling, you get less money back. Lastly, there's also the risk of rating downgrades, and this might happen because bonds are assigned credit ratings (to understand how creditworthy their issuers are and how likely they are to default). Rating agencies are the ones that attribute these ratings based on the issuer's creditworthiness (usually their history of default). Now, if a rating agency downgrades a bond issued by a corporation, this means that the issuer's (in this case, the corporation's) credit quality falls, which at the same time increases the risk of default. This often leads to a decrease in the bond's price and might have an impact on your returns.

Understanding all of these risks is important for you, the investor, to pick your bonds and be able to create a sound strategy where you not only get good returns but also mitigate your risks.

HOW BONDS FIT INTO YOUR INVESTMENT PORTFOLIO

From an investor's point of view, bonds are a great way to diversify your portfolio and, with that, mitigate the risk of investment. At your age, as a young investor, understanding how bonds fit into your portfolio is vital to maximizing your returns. In other words, you can use bonds to complement your investment strategy based on some of the following factors.

Your age, for instance, is one of the factors. At this early stage in your life, you have a longer investment horizon, which means that your money is in the market for longer and has more chances of growing. This longer timeframe allows you to take higher risks and potentially reach better returns. Your investment goals are also an important factor, and many teens prefer to maximize their capital growth. Here, bonds can play an important role, especially higher-yield bonds that have higher interest rate returns.

You also have to consider the investment horizon that I mentioned above. At this stage, you have a longer investment horizon and more flexibility in your investment choices, such as by choosing bonds with longer maturities. Last but not least, you should also consider your risk tolerance. Usually, the younger you are and the longer your time horizon is, the higher your risk tolerance tends to be. However, you should also create a good balance between higher-risk and lower-risk investments to diversify your portfolio and mitigate your overall investment risks.

Other Fixed Income Investments

Alright, so now let's talk about some other fixed-income investment offers other than bonds that can also bring some benefits.

Certificates of deposit (CDs) are time deposits issued by banks and credit unions. Here, you deposit money for a certain amount of time at a fixed interest rate. So, like a mix of savings accounts and bonds, you can pick the maturity period, which can range from a few months to a few years, and accrue interest until the maturity date. When the maturity date is reached, you can withdraw the money deposited and the interest generated during that time. So, the benefits of a CD are that your money is safe, and you get a fixed interest rate. Although your money is locked until it reaches maturity, and you can withdraw it before reaching maturity, you will be penalized. Also, interest rates are often lower than those of bonds. As I've mentioned above, CDs are provided by banks and credit unions, so you can purchase them directly from those institutions either by going to the branch or online.

Money market funds are funds that invest in low-risk securities such as CDs or Treasury bills. These are funds, so investors pool their money, and professional fund managers allocate the money across the different investments to generate income. They are safe, often offer higher interest rates than a savings account, and are another investment you can use to diversify your portfolio.

THE WORLD OF BONDS AND FIXED INCOME INVESTMENT | 71

However, the returns are often lower than those of bonds and stocks. You can get money market funds through brokerage firms or mutual funds, where you can purchase shares of these funds.

Lastly, Treasury securities include Treasury bills, Treasury notes, and Treasury bonds (government bonds, but we've already talked extensively about the latter, so I'm going to focus on the other two). The main difference between these is the maturity time, with Treasury notes maturing from two to 10 years and Treasury bills having the shortest maturity time, from a month to a year. Because of the shorter maturity time, they often offer lower interest rate payments than Treasury bonds. These can be bought directly from the Treasury website mentioned before or in the secondary market.

STOCKS VS. BONDS

Let me give you a side-by-side comparison between stocks and bonds so you can get a better idea (or a simplified look) of how they compare.

	Bonds	Stocks
Type of Instrument	Debt	Equity
Definition	A bond is a debt security, in which the issuer of the bond owes the holder (you) a debt and has to pay interest and repay the principal.	Stocks are issued by businesses to raise capital and sold to investors through company shares.
Holders	As a bondholder, you're lending money to the issuer of the bond.	As a shareholder, you obtain a small percentage of the company.
Issued by	Bonds are issued by companies, governments, and municipalities.	Stocks are issued by companies.
Potential returns	Lower potential returns.	Higher potential returns.
Risk	Lower risk.	Higher risk.

So, as you can see, bonds are a great way to diversify your portfolio investment, even if they tend to offer lower returns. This is because they are usually lower in risk and are great ways to balance your investments. There are many benefits to investing in bonds, such as a fixed income, and some of them are risk-free. Of course, there are risks that you have to consider here, such as interest rate, credit risk, or inflation risk, but just like any investment, you have to do your due diligence before investing, especially when it comes to the bond issuer's creditworthiness. We've also talked about other fixed-income alternatives to investments that might bring some more stability to your investments and diversification to your portfolio.

Most apps that allow you to invest in stocks also have bonds available. For instance:

- Acorn
- Greenlight
- Charles Schwab

In the next chapter, we will discuss other ways to diversify your portfolio while mitigating your investment risks with mutual funds and ETFs.

EXPLORING MUTUAL FUNDS AND ETFS

> *Don't put all your eggs in one basket.*
>
> — MIGUEL DE CERVANTES

The concept of mutual funds and ETFs is intrinsically linked to the quote above from Miguel Cervantes. Even though he was the writer behind Don Quixote, which was written back in 1605, that particular advice is still relevant today. While I'm going to explain these two investment vehicles in detail throughout this chapter, mutual funds and ETFs are a great way to diversify your portfolio. But let's start from the beginning.

WHAT ARE MUTUAL FUNDS?

I've mentioned mutual funds briefly in the previous chapter, but to give you a better definition of them, they are pooled money from different investors. So, every time you invest in a mutual fund, you are buying different bits of an already-existent portfolio. So, imagine that if you buy a share in a mutual fund, within that share, you might have different stocks, bonds, and so on. A fund manager is a person in charge of coming up with this portfolio, and they actively manage it to try to get the best returns to their investors. So, when investors buy shares in a mutual fund, your money is combined with money from other investors like you to create a larger fund (more money). As you might have expected, this is a great way to ensure your own portfolio is diversified because, regardless of how much you invest, you always invest in several different companies, bonds, and so on.

Besides the diversification side of it, investing in mutual funds brings other benefits. For example, most of them are considered low-cost because they not only have a lower investment minimum but also lower fees than directly buying shares individually. If you think about it, it is convenient too because you don't have to manage your own investments, which comes with considerably less time and effort spent. Another thing about mutual funds is that they are usually liquid, meaning that you can buy and sell shares of the mutual fund without much loss and get cash quickly.

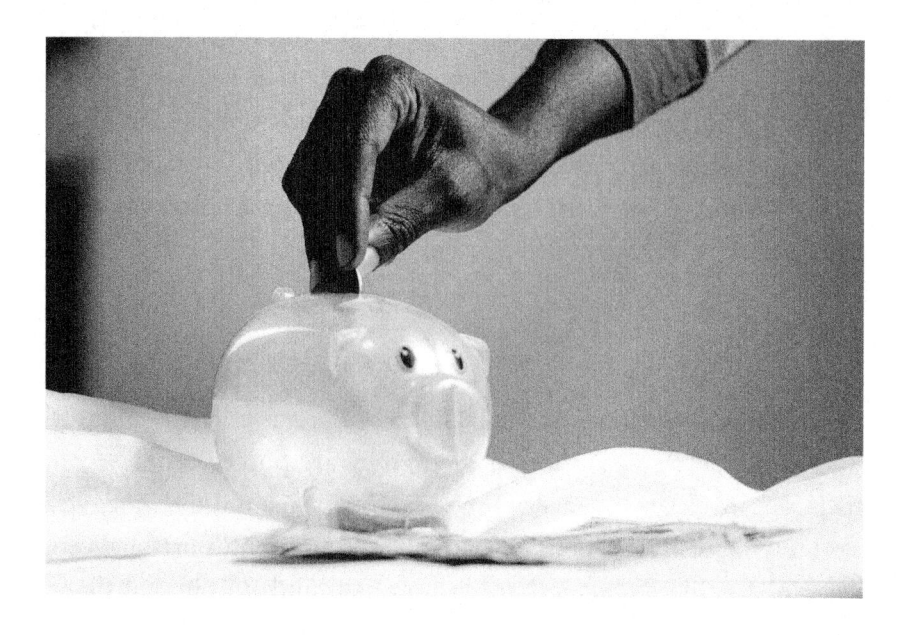

How Do Mutual Funds Work?

Each mutual fund is different and has different investment objectives. This is the only thing you have to do your due diligence on, as well as the fund manager's track record. For instance, if you're looking for growth, you need a mutual fund focusing on growth investments. The same is true if you're looking for an income-type strategy or capital preservation. The fund manager is in charge of selecting the different investments according to their own objectives. Then, investors begin to contribute by purchasing shares of the mutual fund directly from the company that manages the fund or a broker that displays the mutual fund. As you might have guessed, the money the investors contribute is used to buy stocks, bonds, and other securities for the fund portfolio.

Because mutual funds are actively managed, the fund manager is constantly monitoring and adjusting the fund's portfolio based on market conditions to maximize investors' returns. Some mutual funds might be designed for income, and so they pay dividends to their investors just like a dividend stock would. If not, you realize gains only when you sell your shares in the mutual fund.

The Different Types

There are a few different types of mutual funds, each of which tries to meet different requirements and different financial goals, as well as being tailored to different risk profiles.

Stock funds or equity funds have primarily stocks in their portfolio, and the goal is usually capital appreciation over the long term. However, within this category, there are many other sub-types of stock funds that cater to different goals based on many different factors, such as market cap, investment style (such as value, growth, or a mix of both), sector, or even geographic region (such as international stocks).

There are also bond funds, which primarily hold bonds and focus on fixed-income securities like corporate or government bonds. Again, within this category, there's a lot to choose from, and you can further divide them into different factors, such as the credit quality of the bond issuer, the duration of the bonds, and so on.

We've already discussed index funds, such as the S&P 500 or Nasdaq, but keep in mind that fund managers do not actively manage these and, therefore, are cheaper. Money market funds focus on low-risk and short-term investments such as Treasury bills or CDs.

Asset allocation funds focus on a mix of investments, such as stocks and bonds, and are some of the most common types of mutual funds. You can narrow the range of investments and go for sector funds that focus on specific sectors like energy or healthcare, but you'd have less diversification. There are also other, less common funds, such as those based on real estate, commodities, or derivatives, which we will discuss later.

Disadvantages of Investing in Mutual Funds

So, while mutual funds can bring many different benefits to your portfolio, there are some disadvantages to them as well that you have to be aware of so you can make the best possible decisions. One of these disadvantages is the lack of or limited control you have over your investments. This is because fund managers manage mutual funds, and they are the ones who decide what investments to pick. So, essentially, you are placing your money in their hands, and you have to have faith in them and rely on their expertise. Of course, having someone pick the investments for you can be great if you are an investor who doesn't have the time to do their own research, but if you're more of a hands-on type of investor, then mutual funds might not be the best choice for you.

Just because you are relying on someone with expertise doesn't guarantee returns. After all, these are investments, and returns are never 100% guaranteed (unless you solely invest in government bonds). And like any other investment, your potential gains can fluctuate and might underperform. However, keep in mind that you only realize losses if you sell your investments. Even though some mutual funds focus on capital preservation, this still doesn't guarantee returns.

One other disadvantage is fees and taxes, which can be even more bothersome, coupled with the disadvantage above, where you don't make returns. Essentially, with mutual funds, you are paying an expert to pick stocks for you, and, of course, that comes at a cost, which is usually a percentage of the fund's returns. This fee is called an expense ratio and not only helps pay the fund manager but also covers other operating expenses. There are some mutual funds that also charge sales loads, which can also be called commissions, when buying or selling shares from the fund. However, not all mutual funds charge this, and you need to find out if they do when investing in them. There might also be transaction costs when you buy or sell, which are separate fees. Lastly, we have taxes that you might pay on your capital gains, but this is always present in investing, whether using mutual funds or not.

How to Invest in Mutual Funds as a Teen

There are things to consider when you're investing in mutual funds as a teenager. I'll give you a general rundown of the steps you need to go through. The first thing you have to do, and this needs to be done even if you're not a teenager, is to consider your investment goals, risk tolerance, and investment time horizon. We've talked about this extensively; now, you need to apply it before investing in mutual funds. Another thing that has to be done at all times is to pick a fund that is diversified enough; after all, this is the whole point of a mutual fund—diversify your portfolio.

Now, for a specific step for teenagers, or at least those under the age of 18, you will likely need a parent or guardian to set up a custodial account to start investing in the mutual fund. This means that the parent or guardian is the one managing the account on your behalf, at least until you reach legal age. Now, this is not necessarily bad; you just need to know how to work with your parent or guardian to set up this account, and they might even help you pick the best mutual fund for you.

While your parent or guardian manages the account on your behalf, you can still have access to it, which means you should be in charge of monitoring it regularly to check on its performance and progress. At this point, you should also keep track of any fees and any changes in the market.

INTRODUCTION TO ETFS

Alright, so let's get into another type of investment called exchange-traded funds (ETFs). In many ways, ETFs are similar to mutual funds, and because of this, they aim to diversify your portfolio. However, ETFs exclusively trade on stock exchanges, so you can buy them as you'd buy an individual stock, but like mutual funds, they are comprised of many different investments and track the performance of certain sectors, asset classes, or indexes for instance. Much like mutual funds, ETFs also pool their investors' money to invest and diversify their portfolio, but another difference here is that the buying and selling of ETFs can be done throughout the trading day while mutual funds can only be done at the end of the trading day, which is an advantage to ETFs since you can trade them at market prices.

Regarding other distinctions between ETFs and mutual funds, it's also important to highlight their cost and pricing; here, ETFs are cheaper than mutual funds. First, ETFs are passively managed, and as you know, mutual funds are actively managed by a fund manager, so there's no fee to any fund manager when you invest in ETFs. But it's also true that ETFs might incur some commissions depending on the brokerage you use, and mutual funds often don't have commissions on transactions.

One last thing to emphasize is taxes. Here, ETFs tend to be more tax-efficient because of their structure. While I'm not going to get into the details, I will say that ETFs' structure is designed to minimize capital gains.

Advantages of ETFs over Mutual Funds

Let's explore other, more meaningful advantages of ETFs over mutual funds. ETFs, in many cases, have better diversification options than mutual funds because the range of different assets tends to be wider within a single investment. Transparency is also a factor here, and often, ETFs offer more transparency because they divulge their holdings every time there's a change and their respective weights within the portfolio. This way, you, as an investor, can make better choices and assess your portfolio risk much more accurately.

Lastly, ETFs are also more flexible than mutual funds, mainly because mutual funds are priced only at the end of the trading day, while ETFs can be bought and sold throughout the trading day, so you have much better control over your investments.

Disadvantages of ETFs Over Mutual Funds

Now, not everything is better with ETFs, at least when compared to mutual funds. For example, while most ETFs are liquid mainly because they trade on the stock exchange, some might not be as liquid, which makes them have higher volatility, which in turn might make them more costly to trade. On the other hand, most mutual funds have a high level of liquidity.

Now, I think the biggest disadvantage of ETFs when comparing them to mutual funds is their potential lower yields, especially those ETFs that track large sections of the market that might have different or disparate dividend yields, which might bring the whole yield down. Before I go any further, I just need to explain what dividends are. This is a profit payment made by a corporation to its shareholders as a reward for holding the shares and investing in the company. Now, there's another word, "distribution," that is often used interchangeably, but they have different meanings. Distribution is more of a broader term and doesn't indicate only the payment of dividends to investors. This could be a distribution of stocks or bonds instead of cash. When it comes to their tax implications, there's also a difference. Dividends can be qualified or non-qualified, and here, the first is taxed at a long-term capital rate, which is at a lower rate than non-qualified dividends, which are taxed at ordinary income tax rates and so at a higher tax rate. The tax treatment of distributions varies because it doesn't solely relate to dividends but also to stocks, bonds, and so on.

There might also be some tracking errors in some cases, whether it is because of portfolio rebalancing techniques, transaction costs, and so on. Such tracking errors can have an impact on your returns; however, these errors are uncommon, especially if you go for established ETFs.

Of course, while being given the opportunity to trade during the day is great, this can also come with some issues and risks, such as price fluctuations. After all, ETFs are just like individual shares, and the price might go up and down throughout the day depending on supply and demand.

Investing in ETFs

If you're underage, you might need a parent's or guardian's permission to open a brokerage account, which is where you can invest in ETFs. When it comes to picking one, we will talk about it later, but choosing a relatively established brokerage account that offers you a wide range of different ETFs is always preferable.

Before you start investing in ETFs, you need to fully understand the type of ETF you're investing in. As I've said, there are many different types, some focused on certain types of investments or different sectors, and so on. Consider using the average-dollar-cost strategy, where you invest regularly and aim for diversification. And, of course, keep monitoring your performance and making adjustments where you see fit.

MUTUAL FUND VS. ETF COMPARISON

Let's have a look at mutual funds and ETFs side-by-side.

	Mutual Funds	**ETFs**
How are they managed?	Actively managed.	Passively managed.
How are they traded?	Orders for mutual funds are executed only once a day.	ETFs trade like stocks and can be bought and sold throughout the trading day.
What's the minimum investment?	Depends on the mutual fund.	No initial investment required.
What are the costs?	No trading commissions but operating expenses fees.	Some might have trading commissions.
Tax efficiency	Sale of shares might trigger capital gains.	More tax-efficient and often generate less capital gains.

There you have it—a great way to diversify your portfolio and mitigate the risks associated with investing. While mutual funds and ETFs have many things in common, they are not exactly the same, and each has its own advantages and disadvantages. Either way, they both offer great diversification in your portfolio at a good potential return, so it's important to consider them in your portfolio.

When it comes to where you can invest in mutual funds, these are a little harder to find in online brokers, and often, you have to create an account on the financial institution. Here are a few examples of financial institutions that offer mutual funds:

- Fidelity
- Charles Schwab
- BlackRock
- Invesco

In the next chapter, we will look into yet another alternative investment that is completely different from the ones we've seen so far: real estate.

MAKE A DIFFERENCE WITH YOUR REVIEW!!!!

"People who give without expectation live longer, happier lives and make more money."

— FREDDIE MERCURY

Hey there! Do you ever wonder how you can make a difference, even when you're just chilling at home? Well, here's your chance!

Would you lend a hand to someone you've never met, even if you didn't get a pat on the back for it?

Our mission is to make "Investing for Teenagers Made Simple: Your Step-by-Step Path to obtaining Wealth and Financial Freedom Quickly" accessible to every teenager. Seriously, everything I do comes back to that mission. And guess what? I need your help to make it happen.

Most folks do judge a book by its cover (and its reviews). So, here's my ask on behalf of all those teenagers out there struggling with financial literacy, understanding investing, and just generally feeling lost in the money maze:

Could you take a moment to leave a review for this book?

Your review is like a small gift. It costs nothing and takes less than a minute, but it could change a fellow teenager's life forever. Your review could help someone start a business, support their family, find meaningful work, or even help them in a direction to get their dream home.

So, if you're up for spreading some good vibes and making a difference, all you have to do is leave a review. It's as simple as that!

Just scan the QR code below to leave your review:

If you're down with helping out a fellow teenager, you're totally my kind of person. Welcome to the club!

And guess what? I'm super pumped to help you achieve financial independence, accumulate wealth, and gain confidence in managing your money faster than you can imagine. Get ready for some awesome strategies coming your way in the next chapters.

Thanks a bunch from the bottom of my heart. Now, let's get back to our regularly scheduled program!

Your biggest fan,
Riley Wealth

PS - Fun fact: Sharing something valuable with someone else makes you even more valuable to them. So, if you think this book can help another struggling teenager, why not pass it along?

REAL ESTATE INVESTING FOR TEENS

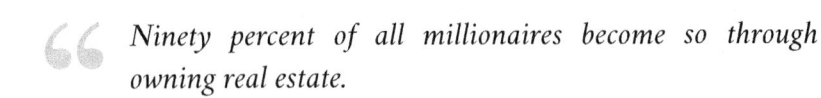

> *Ninety percent of all millionaires become so through owning real estate.*
>
> — ANDREW CARNEGIE

In this chapter, we will look at how you can get started with real estate investments, which comprise investing in properties. Most of the time, investing in real estate is a little more costly than investing, say, in the stock market, but the returns are often a lot higher too.

THE BASICS

Right, so let's start with what exactly comprises real estate. While many people associate real estate with a house, it can also be land or any permanent structures on that land. So it's not limited to a house but any building and even its natural features, such as trees. Real property was given the name to distinguish it from personal property, which is often movable, unlike real property.

Types of Real Estate

Residential real estate is perhaps the most common type of real estate, and the first investors tend to go for it because of its simplicity compared to other types of real estate. So, residential often comprises apartments, family homes, townhouses, and any other type of building where people live. There's also commercial real estate, which is common, too, and these are properties built exclusively for business purposes, such as offices, retail, warehouses, and so on. Industrial real estate has to do with property designed for storage, production, distribution, or manufacturing. So, anything from distribution centers to factories is considered industrial real estate.

There's also raw or underdeveloped land, and this is a plot of land that has nothing in it; it's empty and has no structures. This could be used for future development of real estate, or it could be used for agriculture or anything else. Lastly, there are special-purpose properties, which can come in many shapes and forms and are any type of real estate that does not fit any of the definitions above. These properties are designed for a specific purpose, so stadiums, hospitals, schools, and so on. are all considered special-purpose real estate.

Real Estate Investment Methods

While we will explore this a little more later on, I want to just give you an idea of the main strategies or uses of owning real estate. The first is straight-up direct ownership of real estate for investment purposes, where you can purchase and manage the property to generate income. This often comes in the way of rental income when you rent the property to generate passive income through a tenant paying you rent (this can be done in most forms of real estate).

You can also use a strategy called "flipping," where you buy a property below market value that needs fixing, fix it, and sell it for a higher value and for a profit. Here, you don't rent the property at any time, and the process of buying, fixing, and selling it is relatively quick.

There are also indirect investments, which we will talk about later, that involve not buying a property directly but making smaller investments through real estate mutual funds, real estate investment trusts (REITs), and other avenues.

Risks and Rewards

Like every other investment, real estate has risks and rewards. When it comes to rewards, the potential of a steady income is a great incentive to start investing in real estate. This often comes from rental income. There's also capital appreciation, which often happens with real estate, where the property increases in value as time goes by. When you eventually sell the property, it will generate gains. But like every investment, the longer you hold it, the more you can potentially earn. And it's yet another way to diversify your portfolio, which is completely detached from the stock market, which is great.

Now, there are risks, too, with low liquidity being the major problem here. If you need cash immediately, you can't simply sell your property and expect to have the cash tomorrow; it takes far longer. You need to sell the property, which might take some time, and then wait for the money to come. The location of your property is crucial, and it will define the value and capital appreciation over the years. If the neighborhood improves considerably, you can see higher property appreciation than you would if the neighborhood became stagnant and didn't attract as many people. Also, there's a lot of active management when you own a property and rent it out. While you can always pay for a property management company to do it for you, they would take some of your gains from your property.

How Teens Can Invest in Real Estate

There are different ways that you can start investing in real estate as a teen since it might be difficult for you at this stage in your life to just pay the downpayment on a property. So, house hacking is a great way to start. Here, you'd purchase a multifamily property like a duplex or a triplex and rent out the remaining units while you live in one, not only to help you generate income but also to help you pay the mortgage on the property. Of course, if you're not legally an adult, you'd have to co-sign any agreements with a parent or a guardian. Living in a unit of the property allows you to be considered an owner-occupier, which enables you to get different mortgage rates and the opportunity to learn how to manage a property.

Real estate crowdfunding is a great way to get into the "game" of real estate, and if you're familiar with the concept of crowdfunding, this is when investors pool their money through a crowdfunding platform (such as a website) and, in this case, invest in properties without owning the totality of the property (just a small percentage depending on the amount invested), often not having to deal with management, and still receive part of the rent money. Again, if you're underage, you might only be able to participate if you open a custodial account with a guardian or a parent and invest in crowdfunding real estate projects. This way, you're still investing in real estate without needing a large downpayment investment, so it's a lot lower. There are a few crowdfunding platforms dedicated to real estate, such as RealtyMogul or FundRise, but, as always, you should do your due diligence when looking for a crowdfunding platform to invest in.

Wholesaling is an entirely different way of approaching real estate investment, where you don't necessarily have to own the property and still make an income. So, essentially, you have to look for properties, usually off-market, where the owner is often willing to get rid of the property as quickly as possible. You secure the property under contract and assign the contracts to other investors for a fee, and it is this fee that makes up your income. Negotiation skills are needed, as is understanding the local market well. Also, because you don't pay for the property, you're just securing it and passing it on to another investor (who might purchase the property from the owner), so you don't need a lot of money upfront.

There are specific custodial accounts that your parents or guardian can use to invest on your behalf (if you're a minor) until you reach the age of majority. Examples of custodial accounts are the Uniform Transfers to Minors Act (UTMA) or the Uniform Gifts to Minors Act (UGMA), where you can use the money to invest in all types of real estate.

There are all sorts of creative financing that you can use, and many real estate investors tend to use such strategies over their careers; however, these are often alternatives to the traditional mortgage if, for some reason, you can't get one. For example, with the seller's finance strategy, you negotiate directly with the owner of the property, and they might agree to finance a part of the property or even all of it. A lease option, on the other hand, is when you take over the property for some time with the option to purchase it at a later date at a certain price.

ZEROING IN ON REITS

REITs are yet another way you can invest in real estate at a lower cost than usual. They are very similar to ETFs in that they are companies that own different real estate properties, and you can buy shares from the stock market. These companies also operate or finance properties such as office buildings, residential buildings, resorts, hotels, and so on. Here, investors also pool their funds, and the REIT purchases different investments, which also helps diversify your portfolio. A very particular characteristic of REITs is that they have to distribute 90% of their taxable income among their investors, so they pay dividends, often at a high yield, just like you'd receive rental income from a property if you owned the entirety of it. As you might have guessed, REITs can also focus on different types of properties, some residential, others commercial, and so on.

The Two Main Types

We can divide REITs into two different categories: publicly traded and non-traded. Publicly traded REITs are the ones you can find in the stock market, like the NYSE, and are subject to the same treatment as any other company stock in the market. Because of this, you can buy and sell them as you would with shares of a company. These types of REITs have high liquidity and are transparent regarding the real estate they hold and their price. They are far more accessible than non-traded REITs and offer dividends.

Non-traded REITs, on the other hand, are not listed in the stock market, and the only way to invest in them is privately or if they are offered directly to investors by the company that owes them. Because they are not publicly traded, they have lower liquidity and limited transparency since they are private companies and are not obligated to detail every single piece of information about them; however, they often inform their investors. But it's also true that their potential returns are higher, and with that, they frequently offer higher dividends than publicly traded REITs.

At the beginning of your journey, chances are that you will not come across any non-traded REITs, so for now, you should focus on publicly traded ones and understand them as much as you can before investing.

A disadvantage of REITs, in general, is their tax burden. Because REITs pay dividends, these are often treated as ordinary income and taxed at a higher rate. As with mutual funds and ETFs, you have limited control over what assets you have within these financial vehicles.

Investing in REITs as a Teen

There are ways you can invest in REITs as a teen. For instance, the same way you invest in the stock market through a custodial account. You can find publicly traded REITs with your brokerage account. Alternatively, you can use a custodial Roth IRA or a retirement account (and we will discuss this in the book's last chapter). Retirement accounts are tax-advantaged accounts where you contribute to them, and that money is placed to invest where you can find all sorts of investments, including REITs. The same is true for a traditional IRA, which works exactly the same way, but the way the taxes are paid is slightly different (again, I will discuss these concepts later on).

Tax Implications of Investing in REITs

REITs can come with an intricate set of taxes, but not to worry; I'll go through their most important aspects so you can have a better idea of how this works. As I've previously mentioned, one way to make gains with REITs is through dividends, which are taxed. As you know, REITs are required to distribute a minimum of 90% of their earnings among investors, and these dividends are taxed as ordinary income. So, when you do have REITs and receive dividends, it's common that your broker or financial institution sends you the 1099-DIV form so you can declare the dividends you've received. You might also have to pay capital gains, but this only happens when you sell your shares of the REIT and make a profit, just like you would if you sold any other type of stock. But keep in mind that if you held those shares for longer than a year, then you're taxed as a long-term investment, which is lower than short-term capital gains, which is what you'd have to pay if you held them for less than a year. There are slight differences when it comes to taxing your REIT returns when compared to stocks, ETFs, or mutual funds. Since you receive dividends from REITs, these are often taxed as ordinary income regardless of whether they are qualified or non-qualified dividends because of their unique structure. Often, any dividends from stocks are taxed at a lower rate. However, when it comes to capital gains (when you sell your investments and make a profit), there's no distinction between REITs, stocks, mutual funds, or ETFs.

You might also hold REITs in one of your retirement accounts, such as a traditional or Roth IRA, which, as you know, are tax-advantaged accounts. Depending on your retirement account, these taxes might be deferred (meaning paid later) both on dividends and capital gains.

RECOMMENDED APPS FOR INVESTING IN REITS

Let me give you a list of great apps you can use to invest in REITs. This is not an extensive list, and there are many other apps out there that might fit your investment style better, so it's always important that you do your own research, but nonetheless, this is a good starting point.

Arrived Homes is a new app in the REITs game, but one that has already made an impact. It's a crowdfunding platform, and so you're pooling your money with other investors. The minimum investment is $100, which is great, and their platform is very easy to use. It also offers you a wide range of different real estate investments so you can build a diversified portfolio. Besides that, it gathers a great deal of information that you can use in your research. However, it doesn't offer personalized guidance, which others on this list do.

Elevate Money is also extremely user-friendly, and just like the app above, the minimum investment is $100. While you have a wide range of different investment opportunities, the investment options are limited, especially compared to other competitor apps. Nonetheless, it's a great app if you're just starting out in the REIT world.

FundRise is an app that I've mentioned before and is great for beginners. With a minimum $10 investment, this is one of the cheapest apps on this list when it comes to upfront money invested. It has numerous tax advantages and is the type of app that you can simply set up and forget about while your money grows.

Real estate investing is a great way to diversify your investment portfolio and guarantee a stable income through dividends. Most investors accumulate wealth by investing in real estate, and despite the main form of real estate investment being low in liquidity, its returns can be massive. Here, we looked at the basics of real estate, its different types, as well as the risks and potential rewards. We've also talked about alternative ways of investing in real estate without investing a large sum of money upfront, such as through REITs or real estate crowdfunding platforms.

In the following chapter, we will go through one of the most exciting new ways to invest your money with cryptocurrency and digital investments!

NAVIGATING CRYPTOCURRENCIES AND DIGITAL INVESTMENTS

Cryptocurrency is a new frontier in the financial world—a world that's here to stay. While it is still an emerging technology and investment, it is clear that it is the future, so why not start right now? Even though you might have heard of cryptocurrency, because of how new it all is, it might be a little frightening to know where to start, right? Well, fear not; this is what we will be talking about in this chapter. We will go through what cryptocurrency is, how it can help you financially, and how to start investing in it.

INTRODUCTION TO CRYPTOCURRENCIES

In a basic way, cryptocurrency is any digital currency that is decentralized and used on the internet (so, no physical form). In this case, decentralized means that this type of currency doesn't have an institution or government that controls it in any way. For example, the US dollar is controlled by the US Federal Reserve, which is part of the US government (central banks are another institution that controls currency, like the European Central Bank controls the Euro). They are the ones who dictate its supply and other things that can profoundly affect the value of the currency. With most cryptocurrencies, such as Bitcoin, no one entity controls them. Speaking of Bitcoin, which was launched in 2009, it is by far the most influential cryptocurrency and the one that started this all-emerging field, besides, of course, being the very first successful cryptocurrency. Nowadays, there are others that, even though they have not reached Bitcoin's success, are successful in their own way, such as Ethereum.

So, for an investor, cryptocurrencies are an emergent investment, the future, and an alternative to traditional currencies. To give you a few examples: Cryptocurrencies can now be used for investment, online shopping, and other uses. What's so special about this new digital currency is that it offers things fiat money (traditional currency) doesn't, such as censorship-resistant (from centralized entities) or means to make transfers across the globe without the need for third parties such as banks to help with those transactions, and with that, keeping money more for yourself. This is because these third parties, when it comes to transfers, always take a small percentage to help with the service that is transferring money, even if you're not aware of that fee.

You can also consider cryptocurrencies a speculative investment. Much like stocks, you can buy and sell cryptocurrencies on exchanges and profit from their price fluctuations. However, for reasons that we will explore later, cryptocurrencies are often more volatile than more traditional investments.

Key Cryptocurrency Concepts

There are other benefits that cryptocurrencies bring to the table when compared to fiat currencies. For instance, the transparency that cryptocurrency's underlying technology (blockchain, which we will talk about in the next section) offers. This allows transparent and immutable record-keeping of all cryptocurrency transactions, and everyone can see them. The name cryptocurrency comes from the word cryptography, which is a set of techniques and methods to secure transactions and control the creation of new coins. In addition, we have public and private keys used to authenticate transactions. Privacy is another aspect where cryptocurrencies overperform compared to fiat money. Even if everyone can see all transactions on the blockchain, you don't know who sent them to whom because of the use of pseudonymous addresses and other techniques to mask the users. One last characteristic of cryptocurrency is its irreversibility, which means that once a transaction is made and added to the blockchain, it cannot be undone, which is another layer of security. We can talk about the portability of cryptocurrency, which is certainly useful but not unique to cryptocurrency since fiat money has also achieved that, but with cryptocurrencies, you get transactions completed within minutes, which often doesn't happen with fiat currency, especially if you're transferring funds across the world.

The Technology Behind Cryptocurrencies: Blockchain

As I've mentioned above, blockchain is the technology behind cryptocurrencies. What makes them so special, but how exactly does this technology work?

You can look at blockchain as the underlying infrastructure for these types of currencies that provides them with features such as decentralization and transparency. But let's go through the different parts.

The decentralized ledger of cryptocurrencies is only possible because of blockchain technology. This is a distributed ledger, which means that it is not in one place (or it would be centralized). For example, central banks have a single infrastructure (or network); with blockchain, this infrastructure is divided into many different computers across the globe that form that network. So, for hackers to perform an attack, it would be a lot easier, in theory, to penetrate a central bank network (because it's centralized) than it would be on Bitcoin's network since they would have to simultaneously attack several computers across the globe at once. But I digress a little here, so let's get back to the point at hand. The distributed ledger records all transactions across this network of computers, also called nodes. Each transaction is grouped into blocks, and these blocks are added to a chain (hence the name blockchain) of previous blocks. This creates a chronological record of transactions that is impossible to alter.

While the blockchain is publicly accessible, which means that you and I could see all the transactions and verify them, they are also cryptographically secured and validated through something called a network consensus mechanism, which in Bitcoin's case is called Proof-of-Work (POW), but Ethereum uses a slightly different consensus mechanism called Proof-of-Stake (POS). As I've mentioned, with blockchain technology, there's no need for third parties such as banks to help with transactions because the technology enables peer-to-peer transactions (directly between the sender and the receiver), which also means cryptocurrency doesn't rely on banks or other institutions, which not only reduces the time of transactions but also the cost.

Nowadays, there are many different cryptocurrencies, with Bitcoin being the most popular, but Ethereum is also gaining some ground. However, there are many other smaller cryptocurrencies that are worth mentioning, such as Riple or Litecoin, each with its own unique features.

BUYING CRYPTOCURRENCIES

Buying cryptocurrency is not that different from buying stocks in the stock market. Here, you have two different options: traditional brokers that offer cryptocurrency (although not all do) or dedicated crypto exchanges. With traditional brokers, you will find cryptocurrency listed alongside stocks and other securities. Crypto exchanges, on the other hand, are dedicated platforms where you can buy and sell cryptocurrencies. Often, these exchanges offer you a lot more options than traditional brokerages that offer only large cryptocurrencies. Some of the largest crypto exchanges include Binance and Coinbase. Once you pick the best platform for you (always do your due diligence!) and create an account (the requirements differ with traditional brokerage accounts, which usually request more personal information than crypto exchanges), you have to fund your account so you can start investing just like you would with stocks or any other investment. Here, you will have to fund your account with fiat currencies like dollars or, with some crypto exchanges, transfer existing cryptocurrencies that you hold from your wallet to your account.

Every exchange is different when it comes to transferring your existing cryptocurrency, but it's usually easy, and you just need to follow the steps. Traditional brokerages, as you know, offer different ways of funding, such as debit or credit card payments, bank transfers, and so on, and crypto exchanges often offer similar ways to fund your account.

Right, so now that everything is underway and you've funded your account, all you have to do is place an order. Again, the process might be slightly different depending on the platform you're using, but it often goes something like this:

You pick the cryptocurrency you want to purchase; you choose the quantity you want to buy by entering the amount you want to spend or simply the amount of cryptocurrency you want to obtain (most platforms allow you to purchase fractions as well, which can come in handy). Certain platforms also allow you to set the price at which you want to buy the cryptocurrency, although not all have this feature, or you can execute a market order where you buy the cryptocurrency at the current market price. You will be prompted to review your order and confirm it before actually investing your money, just to make sure you haven't made any mistakes when purchasing. If you're happy with it, all you have to do is confirm your order, and you become the proud owner of cryptocurrency!

Other Ways to Invest

There are other ways you can invest in cryptocurrency that might have less risk. For example, Bitcoin trusts are one of the alternative ways. As you might have guessed, this is focused on Bitcoin, and here, you get exposure to this particular cryptocurrency without directly owning it. These trusts are similar to ETFs, where investors pool money, and the trust invests in them. The same is true for Bitcoin mutual funds, which, in this case, work similarly to traditional mutual funds and are, therefore, managed by fund managers.

If you prefer to invest in blockchain or crypto-adjacent companies, you should look for companies that work with blockchain, whether this is developing the blockchain, mining cryptocurrency (creating), or providing any other ever-expanding blockchain-based services. Also, investing in these companies allows you to diversify your portfolio because many of them work in more established sectors such as technology, finance, healthcare, and so on.

Lastly, you also have the option to invest in blockchain ETFs instead of particular companies. These ETFs would hold blockchain-oriented companies and work just like any other ETF.

OVERVIEW OF DIGITAL INVESTING

Let's now delve into how digital investing works. This is the process of investing in financial markets through an online platform where advanced technology such as artificial intelligence (AI) is at work. What these platforms bring to the table is automation, whether this is in risk assessment, asset allocation, portfolio management, and so on, and helping investors with their decisions. It's often found that these platforms use extremely user-friendly interfaces, which is ideal for beginners. However, these platforms don't solely rely on AI or machine learning; it's an intertwined effort where human expertise is also present to give investors better support in their investments.

Popular Digital Investing Platforms and How to Invest With Them

There are a few popular choices when it comes to digital investing platforms. For instance, Nucoro is a wealth management platform offering automated investments where the platform can come up with customized portfolios based on your own risk tolerance or financial goals. They gather this information through an initial quiz once you sign up. eToro is one of the most popular digital investment platforms and one of the first social trading platforms where they offer a large array of financial instruments, from crypto to stocks or commodities.

However, perhaps the most popular digital investment platform is Robinhood. This is an online trading platform that offers commission-free trades and has many different investment options. Also, its user-friendly interface is appreciated by beginner investors. Another great option is Nutmeg, a digital management service similar to Nucoro, where your choices are important for creating your personalized portfolio.

Digital Investing Benefits and Drawbacks

While convenient and beginner-friendly, there are some risks too. For example, there are a lot of investment options that are available through digital platforms that are volatile, such as cryptocurrencies, far more than you'd find in traditional brokerages. Some digital investment platforms have great security, although not all are like that, so doing your research is crucial. Even the ones I've mentioned above, which are secure, are still susceptible to cyberattacks. Because this is a relatively new field, regulations change fast, which can have an impact on the legality of certain investment opportunities you might come across.

Most of these platforms don't have the proper insurance that you'd have in a more traditional investment account. While some, especially those on the list above, offer some insurance, it's still not as comprehensive as some of the more traditional investment accounts.

Lastly, with any emerging technology, especially online, you must be aware of all kinds of frauds and scams. This becomes more pressing when we're talking about decentralized cryptocurrencies and where there's a high level of anonymity.

But of course, there are a few benefits working for you too. Portfolio diversification is one of them since some of these investments, such as cryptocurrencies, are completely disconnected from traditional investments, and so might not be affected by any market downturn. They also have the potential for really high returns (which come with high risk) and brand-new investment opportunities. All of this can also be a great way to hedge inflation, especially if you manage to get high returns on your alternative investments. And best of all, these platforms are extremely convenient and accessible to all. Usually, all you need is a computer or smartphone and an internet connection.

CHECKLIST BEFORE INVESTING IN CRYPTOCURRENCY

Let me give you a checklist you should use and tick off before plunging into cryptocurrency investment.

What to check before investing:	
Check the project's website	
Read the white paper	
Check social media channels	
Evaluate the cryptocurrency's market metrics	
Determine if the cryptocurrency has a utility	
Check volatility and historical performance	
Check community and ecosystem	
Check regulatory environment	
Analyze the project team and partnerships	

Cryptocurrency is one of the most promising investments nowadays, and it seems that it's here to stay. So, starting to understand how it works and finding out the best way to invest in it might be a great way to guarantee investment returns in the future.

In the next chapter, and with everything we've looked at so far, I think it's time for you to take the first step by making your first investment. Let's see what steps you need to follow.

MAKING YOUR FIRST INVESTMENT

> *The journey of a thousand miles begins with a single step.*
>
> — LAO TZU

In this chapter, we will fully apply everything we've looked into so far as we explore how you can make your very first investment.

Before we get into it, let's just do a quick check of the things you need before placing your first investment (we've been through all of these in the past chapter, so if you have any doubt, just go back and revise):

- Pay off any existing high-interest debt first.
- Use investment apps responsibly.
- Be cautious with crypto and digital assets.
- Resolve to diversify and invest for the long term.
- Secure your online investment accounts.
- Be aware of investment behaviors.

- Choose the right brokerage and account types.
- Fund your account responsibly.
- Pick your stocks carefully.
- Know your investment time frame.
- Establish a plan in relation to investment costs.
- Be patient, and keep educating yourself about investments.

HOW TO OPEN AN INVESTMENT ACCOUNT

Let's, once again, go through how you can open the different investment accounts. While I've mentioned this throughout the previous chapters, here you will have a straightforward and more comprehensive version with some new added details.

Brokerage Account

You need to research and compare the different brokerage companies to find the one that might suit your needs. Remember to check any fees, commissions, trading tools, customer services, and investment options the brokerage firms offer.

Then, you have to complete your application, and this can usually be done by going to the company's website to begin the process. There's usually some personal information that you will need to provide, such as your social security number, ID, and address. Once that is done, you must choose the account type you want. These advantages might depend on the brokerage firm, but the most common is the individual brokerage account. You might also choose from a traditional or Roth IRA or some of the other types of accounts we've talked about earlier (check the previous chapters if you still have any doubts about the different accounts or the last chapter about retirement accounts, such as traditional or Roth IRA).

Then, you just have to fund your account, and here, you will have a few options, too, but this depends on the brokerage you choose; however, bank transfers are usually the norm and available in most brokerage accounts. All that is left is to invest now! Remember to use the brokerage's resources since these can be useful.

ETFs can be bought through a brokerage account in the same way I've explained above.

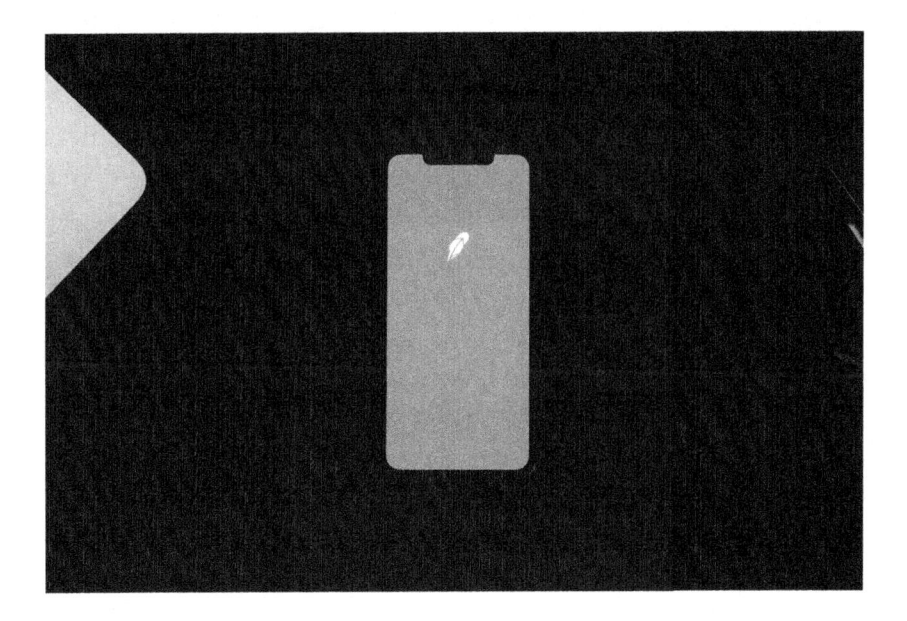

Treasury Bonds

Investing in bonds is infinitely easier (not that opening an account is hard). You can simply go to www.treasurydirect.gov and open an account. All you have to do is follow the instructions, and they will ask you for some personal information, akin to opening a brokerage account.

Mutual Funds

Okay, so there are two main ways to get your hands on mutual funds. One is going directly to the firm that owns the mutual fund or through a brokerage selling mutual funds. Here, you must consider fees, their options, or even customer service. It's also important that you research the funds before investing. Once that is done, you can open an account where, as always, you will have to provide some personal information.

The other way to do this is through an automatic investment plan (AIP). Many different mutual funds offer AIPs where, instead of investing a lump sum of money, you invest a fixed amount; whether it is every week or every month, it's entirely up to you. Then, the process is similar where you need to find the fund you want to invest in, set the contribution amount, which can either be a certain amount or a percentage of your income, schedule these contributions, and that's all. You only have to check if the mutual fund firm allows for AIP.

Bonds

When it comes to bonds, things are similar. If you're looking for Treasury bonds, I've explained how you can invest in the above. If not, there are two ways of doing this. As I've already explained, one is easy: through a brokerage account. Many brokerage firms list bonds, and the process is similar.

The other way is through a bond fund. First, you need to start researching bond funds and checking which one aligns with your needs, much like you would with any other investment. Here, you also have to open an account with a brokerage firm or a mutual fund offering bond funds. The rest of the steps are similar to most of the above.

Specific Guidelines for Teens Under 18

As you know, if you're under the age of 18, there are some restrictions on owning investment accounts, but this doesn't mean you can't own them. To circumvent this, you often have to open a custodial account with either a parent or a guardian, at least until you reach the age of majority. You can still invest through the custodial account, which your parent or guardian manages.

While many brokerage firms offer custodial accounts, Charles Schwab, Fidelity, or Vanguard are popular and a good place to start your research.

UNDERSTANDING FEES AND EXPENSES

As an investor, you need to understand fees and expenses so you know how much they can impact your returns. Let's go through them.

Expense ratios are the annual fees charged by investments such as ETFs or mutual funds, and they're usually related to a percentage of the managed investments. This fee is charged to cover administrative costs, management, and operative expenses. Management or advisory fees are usually found in mutual funds, serve to pay fund managers, and often come as a percentage of assets under management.

Transaction fees occur when you buy or sell securities and are based on the type of investment you're buying or selling. Sales loads are specifically found in mutual funds and are commissions paid to brokers or financial advisers for selling mutual funds. They can come in two forms: front-end loads, which are charged at the time of purchase, and back-end loads, which are charged when shares are sold.

Let's get a little more specific here. Mutual funds charge 12b-1 fees, which are used to cover distribution and marketing expenses; however, these are often included in the expense ratio. Custodian financial institutions charge fees for holding your assets, but you will often see them associated with retirement accounts such as IRAs or 401(k)s.

When you buy or sell a security, like a stock, trading fees are specific to brokerage platforms. Lastly, transfer fees are often charged when transferring assets between different investment accounts.

Now, all of these fees might impact your investment returns, especially in the long run. Even small fees can add up over time and compound to take up a significant chunk of your returns. That's why you need to pay attention to every single fee before investing.

ACTION STEP

If you can, you should incorporate the following steps into your investment strategy before you take the big leap and place your first investment since these considerations might help you mitigate some of the costs:

- Choose low-cost index funds or ETFs with low expense ratios.
- Use no-load mutual funds, which do not have sales charges.
- Opt for commission-free brokerage accounts to avoid trade commissions.
- Consider flat-fee or hourly financial advisors instead of those charging a percentage of assets under management.
- Be aware of and compare the fee structures of different investment platforms.

This is all you need to know before making your very first investment! It's the first step, but an essential one, so you can continue with your journey. We've dove into some of the things we had just brushed through in previous chapters so you can really understand what you need to do and the steps to take before making your first investment.

In the next chapter, we will examine risk management and how you can avoid common mistakes that many new investors make.

RISK MANAGEMENT AND AVOIDING COMMON MISTAKES

> *It's not whether you're right or wrong that's important, but how much money you make when you're right and how much you lose when you're wrong.*
>
> — GEORGE SOROS

It's common that when you start in the world of investing, you might make some mistakes; however, in this chapter, I will go through some of the most common ones so you can avoid them as much as possible, especially by learning some strategies that will help you safeguard your investments.

UNDERSTANDING INVESTMENT RISKS

Let's explore the different types of risks that you might encounter when you start investing. Keep in mind that some of these we've already discussed, but it's always good to revise them.

Systematic Risks

Systematic risks are risks inherent to the whole market instead of a particular stock or sector. Here, you have different subtypes of risks. For example, market risk is the risk of losses because of market fluctuations such as market sentiment and economic conditions. Interest rate risk is also a systematic risk where any changes in the interest rate might affect your securities, especially those with a fixed income, such as bonds. Currency risk refers to changes in foreign exchange rates that might have an impact on your foreign investments if you have any. Inflation risk refers to the risk of increasing inflation that might devalue some of your investments, and equity risk is the risk of losses because of fluctuations in the value of your invested stocks.

Unsystematic Risks

Unsystematic risks refer to sector- or company-specific risks that don't affect the market as a whole. Here, you have business risk specific to that particular business and might have had bad news or a bad financial report. Credit risk refers to losses caused by the failure of a borrower to repay a debt obligation (a default sometimes seen in bonds). Liquidity risk is, as you know, associated with the inability to sell or buy investments quickly or without significant loss of value. Concentration risk happens when your portfolio is not diversified enough and your investments, which are overexposed, take a tumble. Lastly, reinvestment risk occurs when the earnings you get are reinvested at lower rates or yields.

Other Specific Risks

There might be risks that don't fit the two definitions above. To give you a few examples, political risks, for instance, are any losses on your portfolio associated with changes in government policies or regulations. Longevity risks happen more often, and this has to do with the fact that individuals are outliving their retirement savings. Fundamentally, retirees are running out of savings and investments because we are living longer.

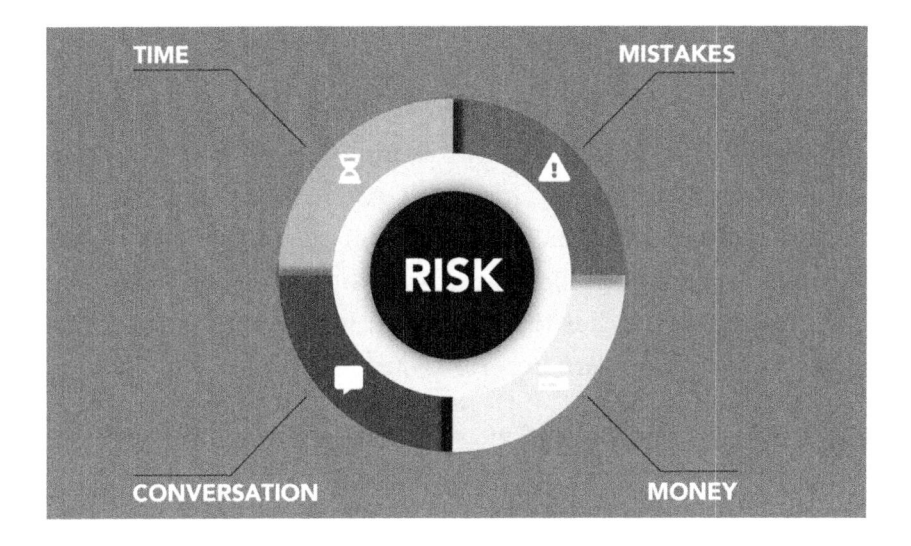

HOW TO ASSESS AND MANAGE RISK

Now that you know the most common risks that you might be facing, you still need to find out how you can assess and mitigate them. This is absolutely crucial to you as an investor so that you can make better decisions. Let's see how you can assess and manage risk.

Risk Management

We've talked about this at the start of the book, so you might be familiar with some of these steps, but the first thing you have to do when assessing risk is to identify your investment goals. This means clearly defining them. Then, you have to determine your risk tolerance, or, as you know, your willingness to tolerate those fluctuations in your investments without deciding to sell everything. You need to consider things such as your financial situation, future income, and, of course, your emotional resilience to the volatility of the market.

It's also important that you fully understand the different types of risks that we've talked about above. After that, you should use risk measures, and here, you will be doing some calculations to quantify the risks associated with investment opportunities. So here, and I'm not going into this too much, you have to assess the standard deviation (a measure of volatility), Sharpe ratio (which is risk-adjusted to inflation), beta (which is the sensitivity to market movements), or value at risk (VaR), which tells you the maximum potential loss over a certain period you could have.

Now, when it comes to managing risk, you already know the basics, such as diversification, asset allocation, or monitoring and rebalancing your portfolio. Another thing that you can use to help you out is using risk management tools and techniques, such as stop-loss orders or hedging strategies. And, of course, always stay informed not only about your investments but also about the market in general.

RISK MANAGEMENT STRATEGIES

Among some of the risk management strategies I've mentioned throughout the book, such as diversification or asset allocation, there are others that can help you manage the inherent risk you find in investments.

Hedging is a particularly great strategy and essentially involves using a strategy to offset potential losses simply by taking an opposing position. Now, you can do this with options, which I will not delve into, but if you are worried about a potential market downturn, you can buy put options on your underlying stock. This means that if your stock goes down, you still offset this loss because, with a put option, you earn if the stock goes down. For example, let's assume for a moment that you own 100 shares of Company X, which is trading at $50 per share. However, you're worried that the stock price will decrease in the following months, but you still believe in the stock and don't want to get rid of your shares. So, you hedge against a potential decline in the price of your stock by buying put options on that same company. The important bit here is that a put option gives you the right but not the obligation to sell a certain quantity of shares of the stock at a certain price (called the strike price) at a specific date (called the expiration date). So, the stock (which we will call the underlying asset) is trading at $50, and the buy-one put option (which represents 100 shares) has a strike price of $45 and an expiration date of three months. So, if, before the expiration date, the stock does fall below the strike price ($45), the option's value will increase, and you have the option to sell your shares at $45, which is higher, limiting your potential losses in your underlying asset. So, if the stock price remains above $45 by the expiration date, the option is said to expire worthless because there's nothing to gain by selling your shares at $45 since the underlying stock is higher, and here you lose the premium (what you've paid for the options). However, if the stock price does fall below $45, for instance, to $40, then you could exercise the put option and sell your shares at a higher price (at the strike price of $45). That's how you hedge against a stock. You can protect yourself from a market downturn and still keep your shares.

Risk transfer happens when you transfer risk that is associated with one of your investments to someone else through an agreement. So, if you transfer your investment to a third party, you can protect yourself. This is exactly what happens when you purchase insurance policies, for example. Risk avoidance is simply not investing in anything that carries risk levels that you are not comfortable with.

Remember that you can always seek professional guidance from financial advisors or any other investment professional since they will give you more personalized advice. Of course, don't forget that continuous learning is important to becoming a better investor.

AVOIDING COMMON INVESTING MISTAKES

Now let's examine the common mistakes many new investors make. Avoiding these is absolutely vital if you want to maximize your earnings and achieve your financial goals.

The first mistake I want to talk about is not understanding the investment. While I've explained the most common investments, you might still have some doubts. However, you can go back and re-read about the different investments. Now, the most common type of this mistake happens with company stocks when you don't fully understand how the company works and how it makes money. You have to conduct a thorough analysis of the company to understand its potential and its risks.

Another mistake that is somehow associated with the above is falling in love with a company. The problem here is that you become biased and allow your emotions to make decisions for you. As an investor, you have to be cold-blooded and think of companies as investments, which is exactly what they are. You have to be objective, and even if a company has this great product or service that you adore, it might not be great from an investment point of view, so you should make a rational decision and either sell it or not invest in it at all.

Of course, one of the most common mistakes is failing to diversify. I've been through this particular problem in other chapters, so this is just to reinforce the idea that diversification is absolutely important for your portfolio. Not only do they diversify across different sectors, but they also diversify across different asset classes, such as stocks, bonds, and mutual funds.

Making emotional decisions is a similar mistake to falling in love with a company, but here, you are not only biased because you really like the company, but you also allow fear or greed to take over your decisions, which is equally bad.

In this book, we aim for a long-term type of investment because that's the strategy that brings the most results, especially if you're just starting out. However, one mistake many young investors make is trying to time the market. When you do this, you are essentially trying to predict short-term market movements, which is far more difficult to pull off. Remember, you are in it for the long term, so you can ride the ups and downs of the market.

Prioritizing investments over other, more pressing financial obligations is also a common mistake. So, things like fixed expenses, debt, or emergency savings are the foundation of good personal finance, and it's important that you focus on them before you set money aside for investments. Chasing trends is something that, unfortunately, many of us do. Investment trends are those stocks that everyone is excited about because they've been going up for a while, and everyone thinks they won't go down. However, more often than not, these investments come crashing down because they've been going up on market sentiment instead of through a logical explanation. You have to do your due diligence and use foundational or technical analysis before making an investment, even if a particular stock is going up and is exciting.

Underestimating the impact investment costs have on your own returns is a big mistake, and I've dedicated a section to this in the previous chapter. Besides fees, you also have to account for taxes, so you must be aware of the different fees you might be charged. Lastly, neglecting the power of compounding is a big mistake because it can exponentially increase your wealth, especially over the long term. The earlier you start investing, the higher your interest will be and the more you will earn.

STRATEGIES FOR SMART INVESTING

Let's just quickly summarize what smart investing strategies look like for you at this point. These are essential if you want to achieve your long-term financial goals. First, you already know this, but you have to understand your financial goals and risk tolerance very well. Then, start with a solid foundation of investments by establishing a good base for your investments and allocating your funds to a diverse array of assets such as high-yield savings accounts (preferably with compound interest), retirement accounts (which we will go through in the next chapter), and index funds and ETFs.

Then, you have to embrace the buy-and-hold strategy, where you hold your investments for years so you give them an opportunity to grow and not depend on the short-term fluctuation of the market. By using this strategy, you're also using the power of compounding. Remember to use dollar-cost averaging by regularly investing fixed amounts instead of a lump sum of money, as this will help smooth out the volatility of the market.

CHECKLIST TO DETERMINE YOUR PERSONAL RISK TOLERANCE LEVEL

Go through this checklist to find out your risk tolerance:

- Assess your financial level, situation, and goals.

  - Identify your investment goals.
  - Consider your time horizon.
  - Evaluate your financial capacity.

- Determine your emotional comfort with risk (how do you react to market volatility?)
- Use tools and questionnaires.
- Consult with a financial advisor.
- Reassess regularly

There are some other questionnaires online that you can use, such as:

- **Investment Risk Tolerance Assessment (University of Missouri):** cafnr.missouri.edu/divisions/division-of-applied-social-sciences/research/investment-risk-tolerance-assessment/
- **Vanguard Investor Questionnaire:** investor.vanguard.com/tools-calculators/investor-questionnaire
- **Edward Jones Risk Tolerance Questionnaire:** www.edwardjones.com/sites/default/files/acquiadam/2021-02/risk-tolerance-questionnaire.pdf

While some of the content in this chapter is more like a revision of what we've talked about in this book so far, it is still important, and there's some new information too. It's crucial that you know how to manage your risk and avoid common mistakes, especially at this early stage in your investment career.

In the next and last chapter, we will be talking about investing and planning for the future, with a special emphasis on your education and your retirement.

INVESTING AND PLANNING FOR THE FUTURE: EDUCATION AND RETIREMENT

Investing is not just about making money. It's about securing your future. This is why it's so important that you think about your education and your retirement savings. We will begin with the education part of it, where we will discuss how you can set up education-related savings accounts before diving into retirement accounts and everything that encompasses that subject.

SETTING UP EDUCATION SAVINGS ACCOUNTS

The aim of education savings accounts is to help you with the burden of college and continuing education costs. I know that a college degree or subsequent education can be pretty expensive, and saving for it can really help you transition to adult life without having too much debt or no debt at all after you're done with your studies. So, let's look at some of the most common education savings accounts.

Most of the following accounts are considered tax-advantaged accounts, which offer tax benefits to those (usually families) who are saving for educational expenses. Essentially, these accounts allow your money to grow tax-free or allow for tax deductions on your contributions.

A prominent education savings account is the 529 College Savings Plan, which is a state-sponsored account that allows families to invest in this account and cover some educational expenses such as books, supplies, or even tuition. Here, any contribution to these plans grows tax-free, and any withdrawals related to educational expenses are also tax-free.

The Coverdell Education Savings Accounts (ESAs) are yet another tax-advantaged savings account that can be used for education-related expenses. They have most of the benefits of a 529 college savings plan with added flexibility when it comes to investment options, such as stocks, mutual funds, or bonds.

The K-12 Education Savings Account is part of the 529 accounts, but it's aimed at families paying for primary and secondary education. It has the same benefits as any other 529 account.

The Benefits of Education Savings Accounts

There are many benefits that come with these ESAs. One that I've pointed out before is tax-free growth, which you can find in all the accounts I've mentioned above. This means that the earnings generated in these accounts are not subject to federal tax, so you don't pay tax on them right away. This allows your money to grow faster, and even if you have to pay tax later on, this doesn't affect the growth.

Many of the accounts I've talked about also allow for tax-free withdrawals, but only if the money is spent on education-related expenses. So, if you use the money in those accounts for any education-related expense, you don't pay tax on it when you withdraw it. Now, not everything education-related falls under the tax-free withdrawal category, but a lot of it does (although this also depends on the ESA you have). Things like tuition, books, fees, supplies, or even computers can be tax-free.

The investments in these accounts are flexible, some more than others, like the Coverdell ESAs, but they all provide you with numerous types of investments to choose from, so you can better build your portfolio and maximize as well as diversify your investments. Because of all of this, you have much better control over your spending and when these funds are spent.

Eligibility Requirements for ESAs

Different ESAs have different eligibility criteria before you, or in this case, your parents or guardians can apply for it. For example, most 529 college savings plans have no age limits or income restrictions, which is of great help to anyone who is trying to get back to studying. The Coverdell ESAs, on the other hand, have a few requirements that you need to meet, especially when it comes to age limits and income. For income, if you're an individual, you can't earn more than $95,000, while if your parents are filing jointly, then the cap is $190,000 in income. Also, contributions can only be made until you're 18 years old, and you have to spend the money before you turn 30 years old. The K-12 ESA has the same limits as the Coverdell ESA.

WHY INVESTING FOR RETIREMENT IN YOUR TEENS?

While you might be wondering why you should be worried about retirement at such a young age, the truth is that the sooner you start, the less you have to worry about in the future. Compounding is a good reason why, as we've discussed in the first chapter. But this is not the only reason why you should. There are also lifelong saving habits that will carry over into adult life. If you develop discipline now, you can establish better habits throughout your life.

It's infinitely more financially flexible and gives you financial security if you start saving and investing now. In other words, you can simply do more things that you enjoy without worrying about your personal finances. As I've mentioned before, tax-free growth, whether in IRA accounts or 401(k)s, can have a significant impact on your earnings.

While I'm going to talk about 401(k)s in the next section, this is a retirement account sponsored by your employer where they match your contributions, meaning they add money to your retirement account too. One last benefit is that retirement accounts often give you legal protection against creditors or lawsuits. This simply means that the money in there is protected against anyone who tries to take it in case you default on your debts.

Investment Options for Teens to Save for Retirement

Before I mention some of the most common retirement accounts, I want to highlight that some of the investments we've been talking about, such as stocks, index funds, and ETFs, including income stocks and value investing, are great alternatives and should complement your actual retirement accounts.

IRAs are individual retirement accounts and a great way for you to start investing your savings for retirement. Here, you have two types, traditional and Roth IRAs, and both are tax-advantaged accounts but work slightly differently. Traditional IRA contributions are pre-tax, meaning that you are taxed as you contribute to the account, but once you withdraw the money during retirement, you won't pay taxes. Roth IRA contributions are after-tax dollars, which means that your contributions are not taxed, and so your money grows tax-free until you withdraw, which is when you pay taxes on them. While both are great ways to save for retirement, choosing between these two comes down to preferences, but with a Roth IRA, your money grows tax-free. You can also contribute to both a traditional and a Roth IRA, but you can't surpass the total annual contributions, which in 2024 will be $7,000 for those under the age of 50.

It's easy to open a traditional or Roth IRA account. First, you need to choose between a traditional or online broker or a robo-advisor (which automates your investments). So, essentially, you need to choose between being more of a hands-on type of investor or not. Then, you will have to pick where to open it; most of the financial institutions I've mentioned throughout the book offer IRAs, such as Fidelity or Vanguard, for instance (although always do your research). To actually open an account, you should go to the provider's website and fill in any personal information they request. It's usually pretty straightforward, and it doesn't change much from opening an account at a brokerage. Then, all you have to do is fund it, which you can do by making a bank transfer.

401(k)s are a little different, and at the moment, you won't have access to most 401(k)s because these are employer-sponsored, which means that you have to work for someone else; however, there are certain financial institutions that do allow you to open one if you work part-time, for instance. The best part of 401(k)s is that the employer matches your contributions, and you can grow your money faster. The maximum contribution, as of 2024, is $23,000 annually. Now, as I've said, the easiest way to open a 401(k) is through an employer, and many companies offer 401(k)s. You cannot open one if you're not working for someone else. The alternative here is IRAs.

Of course, you can always choose high-yield savings accounts, which offer higher returns than regular savings accounts, but these returns are often lower than what you'd receive from a retirement account.

FUTURE SAVINGS CALCULATOR

You can estimate your future savings possibilities through an online savings calculator. Here, you'd add information related to your existing savings, your regular savings amount, for how long your savings will be invested and added interest, and the annual interest rate to find out how much you'd be saving over the years.

While there are many online savings calculators out there, Policy Bazaar has on that is easy to use. The website is the following:

- www.policybazaar.com/financial-tools-calculators/future-savings-calculator/

CONCLUSION

That's it! This is all you need to know when it comes to starting your investment journey right now. Starting early and being persistent are the main takeaways here. It's never too early to begin thinking about your financial freedom, and the earlier you start, the faster it comes. If you start right now engaging with your personal finances wisely and expanding your knowledge, as well as diversifying your investment portfolio, you will be setting a great foundation for the long term.

We began the book by talking about the power of compounding. This is one of the best tools you can use to increase and accumulate wealth, especially if you start now. Before, of course, you need to set your investment goals (all the different types of them), and for that, creating a budget is essential, as is opening a savings account and starting to save for both college and retirement. In Chapter 2, I've emphasized budgeting and saving for your first investment. Here, creating a budget is crucial because you still have to prioritize your needs over your investments. There are plenty of budgeting strategies you can use, and I do encourage you to try a few before settling on one that actually works for you. Besides all of this, you can't forget your emergency fund, which should be a priority. Remember, this is a financial cushion that you can use if unexpected expenses come your way and you don't want to touch your savings or investments.

In Chapter 3, we moved on to actual investments and how the stock market works. The stock market is the place where you can potentially earn more returns, but it comes with a higher risk, so it's imperative that you do your due diligence on every single stock you invest in and, of course, diversify! Here, we went through the basics, the different types, and how dividends work, among other things.

Then, we continued to move on to alternative investments, which are a great source of diversification, and in this case, bonds can also bring you a more stable income. We looked at how bonds can increase your wealth and your income, the different types there are, and how you can incorporate them into your portfolio. Besides that, there are other alternative fixed-income investments, such as CDs or money market funds, that can help you diversify your investments. We've also talked about mutual funds and ETFs and how these are king when it comes to diversification. Real estate, while traditionally requiring a large investment, can really increase your wealth both through rental income and appreciation. However, there are other ways to invest in real estate that cost a little less, such as through REITs or crowdfunding. We also talked about a fascinating and emerging investment: cryptocurrencies. This is what the new economy will look like, and they are here to stay. However, at the moment, they are volatile, and any investment should be carefully considered.

Once all of the necessary information was out of the way, I dedicated a chapter to making your first investment and went through all the checks you have to go through before venturing into the investment world. In Chapter 9, we talked about risk management and how you can avoid common mistakes that many young investors fall into. In the last chapter, we talked about how to invest and plan for the future through education and retirement, two essential aspects of your finances. Here, we went through the most common accounts and how to open them so you can start thinking about your future right away.

There's no more basic or foundational aspect I have to tell you about. Now that you have all the necessary tools to succeed, it's time that you put your knowledge into action. Whether it's buying your first stock, creating a budget, or opening a savings account, the important thing is that you start building your financial future today!

REVIEW REQUEST!!!!

Now that you've got all the tools to achieve financial independence, accumulate wealth, gain confidence in money management, and understand financial markets, it's time to pay it forward and help others do the same.

By sharing your honest opinion of this book on Amazon, you're not only letting other teenagers with limited financial literacy, understanding of investing principles, fear of making financial mistakes, or limited access to investment resources know where they can find the help they need, but you're also spreading the passion for investing among your peers.

Thank you for your contribution. The Investing for Teens community thrives when we share our knowledge and experiences, and you're playing a crucial role in keeping that momentum going.

Scan the QR code below to leave a review.

Keep shining bright, and let's continue empowering teenagers to take charge of their financial futures!

Your biggest fan,
Riley Wealth

GLOSSARY

Asset allocation: This is the process of distributing your investments through different asset classes, such as stocks, bonds, and mutual funds, so you can create a balance between risk and return in your portfolio.

Beta: This refers to a measure of a stock's volatility when compared to the market. It essentially tells you how sensitive the stock is to market movements.

Bond: This is a fixed-income investment, which in reality is a loan made by the government or a company to an investor (the lender).

Brokerage account: This is an account you can open with a brokerage company that allows you to buy or sell securities like stocks, mutual funds, and bonds.

Compound interest: This refers to interest calculated on the initial principal, which also accumulates interest throughout prior periods.

Diversification: This is a strategy that refers to the spreading of investments across different sectors and asset classes to mitigate risk.

Distribution: This refers to a payment made by an ETF, REIT, or mutual fund to their shareholders, which can be in the form of cash or additional shares.

Dividend: This refers to a payment made to investors by a corporation to its shareholders based on the surplus of profit made by the company.

ETF: This refers to an exchange-traded fund, which is a type of investment fund in the stock market that holds bonds and stocks, among other investments.

Expense ratio: This is the annual fee charged by mutual funds to cover operating expenses.

Fiat currencies: This refers to the traditional form of money, such as dollars or euros, issued by a centralized entity such as a central bank or a government.

Hedging: This refers to a risk management strategy to offset potential losses in an investment by betting against your existing investment.

Index funds: This refers to either an ETF or a mutual fund that often aims at replicating the performance of a certain segment of the market.

Interest rate risk: This refers to the changes in interest rates that might affect the value of your investments.

Investment horizon: This is the length of time an investor expects to hold an investment before selling it.

Liquidity: This refers to how easy it is for you to convert an investment into cash without losing too much value.

Mutual fund: This is an investment vehicle where investors pool their money, and the fund manages to invest that money in different types of investments, such as stocks or commodities.

Portfolio: This refers to a basket of investments (from stocks to bonds, mutual funds, etc.) owned by an investor.

Risk tolerance: This is the degree of uncertainty an investor is willing to go through for potential returns.

Stock: This is one of many types of securities and represents a percentage of the ownership of a business.

Volatility: This is a measure of the fluctuance of the market or individual stocks.

REFERENCES

Artzberger, W. (2023, December 24). *Avoid these 8 common investing mistakes.* Investopedia. https://www.investopedia.com/articles/stocks/07/beat_the_mistakes.asp

Asset allocation and diversification. FINRA. https://www.finra.org/investors/investing/investing-basics/asset-allocation-diversification

Benzinga Contributors. (2023, November 3). *Best real estate investing apps in 2024.* Benzinga. https://www.benzinga.com/money/best-real-estate-investing-apps

Boyte-White, C. (2022, October 30). *How to buy mutual funds online.* Investopedia. https://www.investopedia.com/articles/investing/111915/looking-buy-mutual-funds-online-here-how.asp

Bromberg, M. (2024, March 24). *Investing for teens: What they should know.* Investopedia. https://www.investopedia.com/investing-for-teens-7111843

Butler, C. (2022, May 8). *Risk tolerance.* Investopedia. https://www.investopedia.com/articles/pf/07/risk_tolerance.asp

Compound interest calculator. (n.d.). The Calculator Site. http://www.thecalculatorsite.com/finance/calculators/compoundinterestcalculator.php

Chen, J. (2023, May 9). *Time horizon.* Investopedia. https://www.investopedia.com/terms/t/timehorizon.asp

EconEdLink - compound interest calculator. (2021, May 15). EconEdLink. http://econedlink.org/resources/compound-interest-calculator/

Fernando, J. (2024, Februay 28). *The power of compound interest: Calculations and examples.* Investopedia. https://www.investopedia.com/terms/c/compoundinterest.asp

Free budget templates | Microsoft create. (n.d.). Create.microsoft.com. http://create.microsoft.com/en-us/templates/budgets

Gillespie, P. (2015, April 28). *Meet the 17-year-old investor who tripled his money.* CNNMoney. https://money.cnn.com/2015/04/28/investing/millennial-investor-17-year-old-brandon-fleisher/

Gravier, E. (2024, March 6). *Financial advisors agree: These are the 3 best investing tips for beginners.* CNBC. https://www.cnbc.com/select/investing-tips-for-beginners/

Hayes, A. (2023, December 2). *Basic investment objectives.* Investopedia. https://www.investopedia.com/managing-wealth/basic-investment-objectives/

Investment risk tolerance assessment // college of agriculture, food and natural resources.

(2024). Cafnr.missouri.edu. http://cafnr.missouri.edu/divisions/division-of-applied-social-sciences/research/investment-risk-tolerance-assessment/4

Kenton, W. (2022, July 12). *Risk assessment definition, methods, qualitative vs. quantitative*. Investopedia. https://www.investopedia.com/terms/r/risk-assessment.asp

Lin, N. (2023, September 6). *Most teens interested in investing, few have started, fidelity reports*. Planadviser. https://www.planadviser.com/teens-interested-investing-started-fidelity-reports/

Lioudis, N. K. (2022, September 27). *How does an investor make money on bonds?* Investopedia. https://www.investopedia.com/ask/answers/how-does-investor-make-money-on-bonds/

Mitra, M. (2020, November 23). *Meet the teens saving for retirement*. Money. https://money.com/teenagers-retirement-savings-roth-ira/

O'Shea, A. (2024, January 30). *How to open an IRA in 4 steps*. NerdWallet. https://www.nerdwallet.com/article/investing/how-and-where-to-open-an-ira

Ren, C. (2023, October 12). *Where do bonds fit in an investment portfolio?* Business Research and Insights. https://business.nab.com.au/where-do-bonds-fit-in-an-investment-portfolio/

Risk tolerance questionnaire. (n.d.). http://www.edwardjones.com/sites/default/files/acquiadam/2021-02/risk-tolerance-questionnaire.pdf

Royal, J., & Durana, A. (2024, February 20). *How to buy bonds: A step-by-step guide for beginners*. NerdWallet. https://www.nerdwallet.com/article/investing/how-to-buy-bonds

Soares, X. (2023, May 11). *7 key ways to evaluate a cryptocurrency before buying it*. Coin Desk. https://www.coindesk.com/learn/7-key-ways-to-evaluate-a-cryptocurrency-before-buying-it/

Stawski, B, & Gravier, E. (2024, April 1). *These are the best teen checking accounts of april 2024*. CNBC. https://www.cnbc.com/select/best-teen-checking-accounts/

Taylor, B. (2022, September 26). *The costs of investing*. Investopedia. https://www.investopedia.com/investing/costs-investing/

Tritsch, E. (2022, January 1). *How to set goals for teens - the SMART goals method*. Fairborn Digital Academy. https://fairborndigital.us/2022/01/01/smart-goals-for-teens/

Waugh, E. (2022, April 11). How to set SMART financial goals - experian. *Experian*. https://www.experian.com/blogs/ask-experian/how-to-set-smart-financial-goals/

Williams, R. (2023, March 2). *Saving for college: Coverdell education savings accounts*. Charles Schwab. https://www.schwab.com/learn/story/saving-college-coverdell-education-savings-accounts

Your stage of life. (n.d.). Project Invested. https://www.projectinvested.com/markets-explained/your-stage-of-life/

IMAGES

Akyurt, E. (2018). Black and white dartboard. In *Pexels*. https://www.pexels.com/photo/black-and-white-dartboard-1552617/

Branco, M. (2018). Three round silver-and-gold-colored coins. In *Pexels*. https://www.pexels.com/photo/three-round-silver-and-gold-colored-coins-1263324/

energepic. (2016). Close-up photo of monitor. In *Pexels*. https://www.pexels.com/photo/close-up-photo-of-monitor-159888/

Kamornboonyarush, A. (2018). Photo of person holding alarm clock. In *Pexels*. https://www.pexels.com/photo/photo-of-person-holding-alarm-clock-1028741/

McBee, D. (2018). High angle shot of suburban neighborhood. In *Pexels*. https://www.pexels.com/photo/high-angle-shot-of-suburban-neighborhood-1546168/

Mellish, B. (2016). House lights turned on. In *Pexels*. https://www.pexels.com/photo/house-lights-turned-on-106399/

Miroshnichenko, T. (2021). Close-Up shot of a person holding a tablet. In *Pexels*. https://www.pexels.com/photo/close-up-shot-of-a-person-holding-a-tablet-6913327/

Neel, A. (2021). Robinhood open screen. In *Pexels*. https://www.pexels.com/photo/apple-iphone-desk-laptop-6633921/

Nekrashevich, A. (2021a). Buy, hold, sell. In *Pexels*. https://www.pexels.com/photo/business-paper-finance-decision-6801651/

Nekrashevich, A. (2021b). Stock market paper. In *Pexels*. https://www.pexels.com/photo/person-hands-pen-glass-6801681/

Piacquadio, A. (2020a). Crop businessman giving contract to woman to sign. In *Pexels*. https://www.pexels.com/photo/crop-businessman-giving-contract-to-woman-to-sign-3760067/

Piacquadio, A. (2020b). Confident senior businessman holding money in hands while sitting at table near laptop. In *Pexels*. https://www.pexels.com/photo/confident-senior-businessman-holding-money-in-hands-while-sitting-at-table-near-laptop-3823493/

Pickens, J. (2020). Person putting coin in a piggy bank. In *Pexels*. https://www.pexels.com/photo/person-putting-coin-in-a-piggy-bank-3833052/

Pixabay. (n.d.). Black calculator near ballpoint pen on white printed paper. In *Pexels*. Retrieved February 29, 2016, from https://www.pexels.com/photo/black-calculator-near-ballpoint-pen-on-white-printed-paper-53621/

Pixabay. (2016a). Person holding debit card. In *Pexels*. https://www.pexels.com/photo/person-holding-debit-card-50987/

REFERENCES

Pixabay. (2016b). Books in black wooden book shelf. In *Pexels*. https://www.pexels.com/photo/books-in-black-wooden-book-shelf-159711/

Production, M. (2020). Risk management chart. In *Pexels*. https://www.pexels.com/photo/risk-management-chart-5849593/

rimthong, maitree. (2018). Person putting coin in a piggy bank. In *Pexels*. https://www.pexels.com/photo/person-putting-coin-in-a-piggy-bank-1602726/

Vaitkevich, N. (2020). Black remote control beside silver round analog wall clock. In *Pexels*. https://www.pexels.com/photo/black-remote-control-beside-silver-round-analog-wall-clock-6120218/

Worldspectrum. (2018). Ripple, etehereum and bitcoin and micro sdhc card. In *Pexels*. https://www.pexels.com/photo/ripple-etehereum-and-bitcoin-and-micro-sdhc-card-844124/

Printed in Great Britain
by Amazon